Parent-to-Child Instruction on Human Sexuality

A Guide for Parents

The principle of decency must safeguard the virtue of Christian chastity. Therefore, in passing on sexual information in the context of education for love, the instruction must always be "positive and prudent," (*Gravissimum Educationis*, 1) and "clear and delicate," (*Familiaris Consortio*, 37).

These four words used by the Catholic Church exclude every form of unacceptable content in sexual education. [For example, (a) visual erotic material; (b) written or verbal erotic presentations (cf. "Educational Guidance in Human Love," 76); (c) obscene or coarse language; (d) indecent humor; (e) the denigration of chastity; and (f) attempts to minimize the gravity of sin against this virtue.]

— *The Truth and Meaning of Human Sexuality,* Pontifical Council for the Family, §126.

Parents: This booklet is not intended to be read verbatim in its entirety to a child at any particular age. It is certainly not intended to be given to children for their own reading.

Use this booklet as a resource to help you explain human sexuality and Catholic teaching.

Be sure to read the "Message to Parents" on page iii.

Publisher
Foundation for the Family, Inc.

Editor-in-Chief
Keith Bower

Mailing address
P.O. Box 111184
Cincinnati, OH 45211
U.S.A.

Telephone: (513) 471-2000
(513) 557-2449 FAX

Nihil obstat

Reverend Ralph J. Lawrence
3 June 1996

Imprimatur

Most Reverend Carl K. Moeddel
Vicar General and Auxiliary Bishop of the Archdiocese of Cincinnati
10 June 1996

The *Nihil obstat* and the *Imprimatur* are a declaration that a book or pamphlet is considered to be free from doctrinal or moral error. It is not implied that those who have granted the *Nihil obstat* and *Imprimatur* agree with the contents, opinions, or statements expressed.

This curriculum has passed both the Consistency Review and the Conformity Review of the Office for the Catechism, National Conference of Catholic Bishops.

Cataloging data
Dewey:
Library of Congress: 96-084266
ISBN: 0-926412-15-9

Foundation for the Family, Inc.
Parent-to-Child Instruction on Human Sexuality

First Edition, Third Printing: 7,000, January, 2000

Message to Parents

We designed this booklet to help parents establish a dialogue with their children concerning human sexuality. The topics covered are not appropriate for discussion or treatment in a classroom, same-sex or mixed.

No one can dictate when you should discuss any of these topics with your child. It is impossible for a curriculum designer to know when a particular child will reach the age at which a certain topic should be brought up. Much depends on the dialogue you have already established with your child. Much also depends on the standards of modesty that pertain to your household.

Some parents may decide to impart some of this information before another parent would deem appropriate. That is their decision to make. Our advice: discern when your child seems ready to hear what you have to say.

These talks are "sample talks." They are intended to provide clear and concise wording on matters of sexuality. The "talks" may not suit the level of vocabulary or psychosexual development of a particular child. They are meant not only to provide information but also to encourage parents to look at how they might rephrase things in their own language. Consider these talks as "first drafts" of your own advice on these subjects. The process of rephrasing someone else's remarks will help you refine how you can best communicate the miracle of procreation and the splendor of the Church's truth concerning human sexuality.

If you determine that your child has not yet reached the age for imparting this information, we still encourage you to start a private dialogue with your child. Get familiar with the child, talking about subjects that currently interest him or her. Work at keeping eye contact with your child to build trust and intimacy between you. The goal is to make it natural for your child to turn to you when the perplexing questions about human sexuality or other issues arise.

Whatever your decision about age-appropriateness, please review the lessons of Grade Six. Some parents may decide that the discussions and exercises of this grade may be beneficial to their children, even though they have not formally had a "talk" about human sexuality. Children are remarkable listeners and learn from our actions and emotional responses as well as from our words. It may be that your child already understands enough to participate in classroom activities concerning the virtue of chastity without having the private dialogue introducing the facts of life.

Should you decide to forego the Grade Six lessons, it may be possible to "catch up" at home prior to Grade Seven, or even Grade Eight. The concepts in these lessons, the import of the scriptures used, and the examples used are all explained with the prospect that the "teacher" involved may be the parent in the home, not necessarily a classroom instructor or catechist. After all, the parent is always the primary teacher.

The perversions of human sexuality, as the Pontifical Council for the Family notes, should not be part of the dialogue with your children unless knowledge of such things has intruded upon them from peers or the surrounding culture. It is because of these unfortunate and untimely intrusions that the materials concerning homosexuality, sexually transmitted diseases, and unchaste sexuality in general have been included.

These are particularly difficult subjects for parents to discuss since our natural modesty would rather shun them. If your child gives signs of being perturbed or curious about such subjects, your responsibility is to place these things in the context of your faith and prevent confusion about the teaching of the Church. We suggest that the best way to do this is to make frequent reference to the *Catechism of the Catholic Church*, personally searching those sections that pertain to any area in which questions arise. After discernment and prayer, explain what the Church is saying about the subject.

We have fashioned explanations that we believe clearly convey the mind of the Church on these subjects. We hope that this will help you deal with these matters prudently and delicately. Remember that God has given you the graces of the sacrament of marriage to help you in educating your child for sanctity. Pray daily for the guidance of the Holy Spirit and for the chastity of your children.

— The Publisher

The following three pages are intended to help you understand the importance of the work you are about to undertake in introducing your child to human sexuality.

"A Primary and Inalienable Right and Duty" on the next page is an invitation to embrace this sacred task that is owed in justice to the young. The teaching of the Church is clear about the fundamental right and duty of parents in this matter.

The next two pages are excerpts from an important Vatican document. We had intended to write our own introduction on imparting this information to the child who has reached puberty, but in the meantime the Pontifical Council for the Family released ***The Truth and Meaning of Human Sexuality: Guidelines for Education within the Family***, dated December 8, 1995.

This document far surpasses anything we might have to say in helping you teach your child in the most prudent fashion according to the mind of the Church. Our excerpts are from the section titled "Four Principles regarding Information about Sexuality," and the section specific to puberty "Principal Stages of Development."

It is strongly recommended that all those concerned with the proper teaching of human sexuality to young people read the complete text of this document.

A Primary and Inalienable Right and Duty

PARENTS are the primary educators of their children, particularly in matters related to sexuality. This right is given to them by God, Who also assigns to parents a duty to teach Christian morality to their children.

God, the Author of life, invites parents to join in the creative process of generating new human life. The role of parents continues as guardians and caretakers of the gift of a child.

"The right and the duty of parents to educate their children are primordial and inalienable" (CCC: 2221).

"As it is the parents who have given life to their children, on them lies the gravest obligation of educating their family. They must therefore be recognized as being primarily and principally responsible for their education. The role of parents in education is of such importance that it is almost impossible to provide an adequate substitute.... The family is therefore the principal school of the social virtues which are necessary to every society" (Vatican II, *Gravissimum Educationis*, §3).

A human being's sexuality cannot be separated from who he is as a person. The responsibility of parents to steer the discipline and development of a child involves the child's total development, including his sexual morality. (Cf. "Educational Guidance in Human Love," §37.)

Parents are called to give their children "a clear and delicate" sex education, one that is "truly and fully personal" (John Paul II, *Familiaris Consortio,* §37).

"Sex education, which is a basic right and duty of parents, must always be carried out under their attentive guidance, whether at home or in education centers chosen and controlled by them" (ibid).

"...Education for chastity is absolutely essential, for it is a virtue that develops a person's authentic maturity and makes him or her capable of respecting and fostering the 'nuptual meaning' of the body. Indeed Christian parents, discerning the signs of God's call, will devote special attention and care to education in virginity or celibacy as the supreme form of that self-giving that constitutes the very meaning of human sexuality" (ibid).

Sexuality is interconnected with morality and spirituality; therefore, sex education cannot be taught apart from Christian principles. To "love the Lord your God with all your heart, soul, and mind" includes all of oneself.

The Church reaffirms the law of subsidiarity. This means those in higher authority must respect the rights of those in lower authority. If some matter can and should be handled within the home, it is wrong to usurp the family's right to take care of it at that level.

A school that cooperates in the sex education of a child should enter "into the same spirit that animates the parents" (ibid). Schools play an important role in supporting the parents' cultivation of virtue in their children.

Yet, when it comes to discussing sexual matters beyond the abstract (that is, in any detailed or descriptive way), the classroom or other public setting is not the appropriate place.

The family is "the school of richest humanity. It is, in fact, the best environment to accomplish the obligation of securing a gradual education in sexual life. The family has an affective dignity which is suited to making acceptable without trauma the most delicate realities and to integrating them harmoniously in a balanced and rich personality.... The fact remains ever valid that with regard to the more intimate aspects, whether biological or affective, an individual education should be bestowed, preferably within the sphere of the family" ("Educational Guidance in Human Love," §§ 48, 58).

Further, regardless of their professional credentials, parents are best suited to be the primary educators of their children. Their loving relationship with their offspring is singular and irreplaceable and therefore cannot be delegated to others or usurped by others. (Cf. "Educational Guidance," §87.)

"There can be no avoiding the duty to offer, especially to adolescents and young adults, an authentic education in sexuality and in love, an education that involves *training in chastity*" (John Paul II, *Evangelium Vitae,* §97).

If parents do not feel comfortable speaking to their children regarding sexual issues, they have a responsibility to seek the resources to learn how better to handle such matters. This booklet is offered as a resource for assisting parents in presenting such information. ■

Excerpts from *The Truth & Meaning of Human Sexuality*

Four Principles Regarding Information about Sexuality

65. 1. **Each child is a unique** and unrepeatable person and must receive individualized formation. Since parents know, understand and love each of their children in their uniqueness, they are in the best position to decide what the appropriate time is for providing a variety of information, according to their children's physical and spiritual growth. No one can take this capacity for discernment away from conscientious parents....

66. Each child's process of maturation as a person is different. Therefore, the most intimate aspects, whether biological or emotional, should be communicated in a personalized dialogue.... In their dialogue with each child, with love and trust, parents communicate something about their own self-giving which makes them capable of giving witness to aspects of the emotional dimension of sexuality that could not be transmitted in other ways.

67. Experience shows that this dialogue works out better when the parent who communicates the biological, emotional, moral and spiritual information is of the same sex as the child or young person. Being aware of the role, emotions and problems of their own sex, mothers have a special bond with their daughters, and fathers with their sons. This natural bond should be respected. Therefore, parents who are alone will have to act with great sensitivity when speaking with a child of the opposite sex, and they may choose to entrust communicating the most intimate details to a trustworthy person of the same sex as the child. Through this collaboration of a subsidiary nature, parents can take advantage of expert, well-formed educators in the school or parish community, or from Catholic associations.

68. 2. **The moral dimension**must always be part of their explanations. Parents should stress that Christians are called to live the gift of sexuality according to the plan of God who is Love, i.e., in the context of marriage or of consecrated virginity and also celibacy.... They must insist on the positive value of chastity and its capacity to generate true love for other persons. This is the most radical and important moral aspect of chastity. Only a person who knows how to be chaste will know how to love in marriage or in virginity....

...70. 3. **Formation in chastity** and timely information regarding sexuality must be provided in the broadest context of education for love. It is not sufficient, therefore, to provide information about sex together with objective moral principles. Constant help is also required for the growth of children's spiritual life, so that the biological development and impulses they begin to experience will always be accompanied by a growing love of God, the Creator and Redeemer, and an ever greater awareness of the dignity of each human person and his or her body. In the light of the mystery of Christ and the Church, parents can illustrate the positive values of human sexuality in the context of the person's original vocation to love and the universal call to holiness.

71. Therefore, in talks with children, suitable advice should always be given regarding how to grow in the love of God and one's neighbor, and how to overcome any difficulties: "These means are: discipline of the senses and the mind, watchfulness and prudence in avoiding occasions of sin, the observance of modesty, moderation in recreation, wholesome pursuits, assiduous prayer and frequent reception of the Sacraments of Penance and the Eucharist. Young people especially should foster devotion to the Immaculate Mother of God" (*Persona Humana*, 12).

72. To teach children how to evaluate the environments they frequent with a critical sense and true autonomy, as well as to accustom them to detachment in using the mass media, parents should always present positive models and suitable ways of using their vital energies, the meaning of friendship and solidarity in the overall area of society and of the Church....

...73. The objective of the parents' educational task is to pass on to their children the conviction that chastity in one's state in life is possible and that chastity brings joy....

...75. ...4. **Parents should provide** this information with great delicacy, but clearly and at the appropriate time. Parents are well aware that their children must be treated in a personalized way, according to the personal conditions of their physiological and psychological development, and taking into due consideration the cultural environment of life and the adolescent's daily experience. In order to evaluate properly what they should say to each child, it is very important that parents first of all seek light from the Lord in prayer and that they discuss this together so that their words will be neither too explicit nor too vague. Giving too many details to children is counterproductive. But delaying the first information for too long is imprudent, because every human person has natural curiosity in this regard and, sooner or later, everyone begins to ask themselves questions, especially in cultures where too much can be seen, even in public.

76. In general, the first sexual information to be given to a small child does not deal with genital sexuality, but rather with pregnancy and the birth of a brother or sister. The child's natural curiosity is stimulated, for example, when it sees the signs of pregnancy in its mother and experiences waiting for a baby. Parents can take advantage of this happy experience in order to communicate some simple facts about pregnancy, but always in the deepest context of wonder at the creative work of God....

Children's Principal Stages of Development

77. It is important for parents to take their children's needs into consideration during the different stages of development. Keeping in mind that each child should receive individualized for-

mation, parents can adapt the stages of education in love to the particular requirements of each child....

...87. **Puberty,** which constitutes the initial phase of adolescence, is a time in which parents are called to be particularly attentive to the Christian education of their children. This is a time of self-discovery and "of one's own inner world, the time of generous plans, the time when the feeling of love awakens, with the biological impulses of sexuality, the time of the desire to be together, the time of particularly intense joy connected with the exhilarating discovery of life. But often it is also the age of deeper questioning, of anguished or even frustrating searching, of a certain mistrust of others and dangerous introspection, and the age sometimes of the first experiences of setbacks and of disappointments" (John Paul II, *Catechesi Tradendae,* Oct. 16, 1979, 38; AAS 71 (1979), p. 1309).

88. Parents should pay particular attention to their children's gradual development and to their physical and psychological changes, which are decisive in the maturing of the personality. Without showing anxiety, fear or obsessive concern, parents will not let cowardice or convenience hinder their work. This is naturally an important moment in teaching the value of chastity, which will also be expressed in the way sexual information is given. In this phase, educational needs also concern the genital aspects, hence requiring a presentation both on the level of values and the reality as a whole. Moreover, this implies an understanding of the context of procreation, marriage and the family, a context which must be kept present in an authentic task of sexual education....

...89. Beginning with the changes which their sons and daughters experience in their bodies, parents are thus bound to give more detailed explanations about sexuality (in an on-going relationship of trust and friendship) each time girls confide in their mothers and boys in their fathers. This relationship of trust and friendship should have already started in the first years of life.

90. Another important task for parents is following the gradual physiological development of their daughters and helping them joyfully to accept the development of their femininity in a bodily, psychological and spiritual sense.... Therefore, normally, one should discuss the cycles of fertility and their meaning. But it is still not necessary to give detailed explanations about sexual union, unless this is explicitly requested.

91. **It is very important** for adolescent boys to be helped to understand the stages of physical and physiological development of the genital organs before they get this information from their companions or from persons who are not well-intentioned. The physiological facts about male puberty should be presented in an atmosphere of serenity, positively and with reserve, in the framework of marriage, family and fatherhood. Instructing both adolescent girls and boys should also include detailed and sufficient information about the bodily and psychological characteristics of the opposite sex, about whom their curiosity is growing....

...92. Through a trusting and open dialogue, parents can guide their daughters in facing any emotional perplexity, and support the value of Christian chastity out of consideration for the other sex. Instruction for both girls and boys should aim at pointing out the beauty of motherhood and the wonderful reality of procreation, as well as the deep meaning of virginity. In this way they will be helped to go against the hedonistic mentality which is very widespread today and particularly, at such a decisive stage, in preventing the "contraceptive mentality," which unfortunately is very common and which girls will have to face later in marriage.

93. **During puberty**, the psychological and emotional development of boys can make them vulnerable to erotic fantasies and they may be tempted to try sexual experiences. Parents should be close to their sons and correct the tendency to use sexuality in a hedonistic and materialistic way. Therefore, they should remind boys about God's gift, received in order to cooperate with him "to actualize in history the original blessing of the Creator that of transmitting by procreation the divine image from person to person...." In this way sons will also learn the respect due to women. The parents' task of informing and instructing is necessary, not because their sons would not know about sexual reality in other ways, but so that they will know about it in the right light....

...Positive information about sexuality should always be part of a formation plan so as to create the Christian context in which all information about life, sexual activity, anatomy and hygiene is given. Therefore, the spiritual and moral dimensions must always be predominant so as to have two special purposes: presenting God's commandments as a way of life and the formation of a right conscience....

...96. In answering children's questions, parents should offer well-reasoned arguments about the great value of chastity and show the intellectual and human weakness of theories that inspire permissive and hedonistic behavior. They will answer clearly, without giving excessive importance to pathological sexual problems. Nor will they give the false impression that sex is something shameful or dirty, because it is a great gift of God who placed the ability to generate life in the human body, thereby sharing his creative power with us....

...97. **Since boys and girls** at puberty are particularly vulnerable to emotional influences, through dialogue and the way they live, parents have the duty to help their children resist negative outside influences that may lead them to have little regard for Christian formation in love and chastity. Especially in societies overwhelmed by consumer pressures, parents should sometimes watch out for their children's relations with young people of the opposite sex - without making it too obvious. Even if they are socially acceptable, some habits of speech and conduct are not morally correct and represent a way of trivializing sexuality, reducing it to a consumer object. Parents should therefore teach their children the value of Christian modesty, moderate dress, and, when it comes to trends, the necessary autonomy characteristic of a man or woman with a mature personality. ■

Contents

Human Sexuality for Girls 4
Note to Parents 4
Topics for Girls 7
The Marital Embrace 8
The Gift of Fertility 10
Ovulation and Menstruation 10
Conception, Pregnancy and Childbirth 12
Natural Family Planning in Christian Marriage 13
The Breast 14
Nature's Method of Spacing Babies 15
Health and Hygiene 15
Problems with Menstruation 16
The Bitter Pill 17
Other Concerns 18
Nutrition, Fat, and Fertility 18
Rest and Relaxation 19
Emotional Changes 20
Alcohol and Drugs 20
Masturbation and Homosexuality 22
The Other Half: Male Sexuality 24
The Meaning of Sexuality 25
Contraception and Abortion 27

Human Sexuality for Boys 28
Note to Parents 28
Topics for Boys 32
The Other Half: Female Sexuality 34
The Proper Use of Sexuality 35
What is an Erection? 36
Nocturnal Emission and Masturbation 37
Homosexuality 39
Emotional Changes 40
Alcohol and Drugs 41
A Final Word 42
Contraception and Abortion 44

Occasions of Sin 45
Sexually Transmitted Diseases 46
Glossary 48

Human Sexuality for Girls

Note to Parents

DISCUSSING THE PHYSICAL CHANGES OF PUBERTY often intimidates parents. It can be embarrassing to discuss intimate subjects both because we fear giving a wrong impression about human sexuality and because we have a natural modesty about these matters. Such modesty is a good thing; it is a fruit of the Holy Spirit.[1] A dignified presentation of this material need not be immodest.

This instruction is a parent duty, not a task to be turned over to others.*

****Bold-faced type** is used in passages referring to parental example and responsibility to respect the child's right not to have too much information too soon.*

God is lavish with the graces of the Sacrament of Matrimony. He will provide you, as a parent, all that you need to insure that you will do a good job. Draw on those graces with a short prayer before instructing your child in these matters.

Too often our uneasiness or lack of information about the physical aspects of sexuality obscures our primary concern for the spiritual aspect here. Your child is biologically preparing for parenthood. That will happen naturally all by itself. **What your child needs most is your witness to the dignity of the vocation of marriage.** The example you have given throughout your child's life has been the most important factor in her view of the vocation of spouse and parent.

It is normal to assume that most children will be called to the vocation of marriage, but we must not ignore the possibility of other vocations, such as priesthood, vowed religious life, or dedicated, chaste singlehood. Whether a girl wants to be a mother or a nun, it is important that you give a positive testimony to being a follower of Christ in your role as spouse and parent. This will help children discern more intelligently whatever calling God has for them.

We believe that parents are the best evaluators of when their children are ready for the information that follows. There is much controversy, especially among Catholic educators, whether a "latency period"[†] actually exists. There is encouragement from many so-called "experts" to err on the side of earlier education on sexual matters. "Better five years too early than two minutes too late," some people advise. However, there is no need for early biological information if there is early education in discipleship and Christian chastity.

† The "latency period" is a technical term that comes from the Freudian school of psychology. We use the term here in a more colloquial sense in which it refers to the years before puberty when children have no interest in sexual matters in general and especially have no romantic interest in members of the opposite sex. Another term commonly used for this period is the "years of innocence."

We believe that such a decision is the parents' decision in any case. Catholic educators can serve parents best by advising the need for a talk on detailed sexual matters when they suspect this need from classroom observation.

They can also provide materials, such as this booklet, that will help organize the facts in a manner that also shows the richness and beauty of Catholic teaching concerning sexual morality.

---

[1] The Fruits of the Holy Spirit are good acts whose nature is to give joy to the virtuous. The Fruits of the Holy Spirit are "love, joy, peace, patience, kindness, goodness, faithfulness, gentleness, self-control" (CCC:736, see Galatians 5:22 and 23). The classic listing of these was slightly different: Charity, Joy, Peace, Patience, Long-sufferingness, Goodness, Kindness, Gentleness, Faithfulness, Modesty, Continency, and Chastity. See pp. 313-314 of the curriculum for more.

WHEN IT COMES TO MATTERS OF FAITH, parents are the primary and most influential teachers of their children. A parent who does not consider it an obligation to attend Mass will raise children who fail to take seriously the commandment to honor the Sabbath. A parent's example concerning the Sixth and Ninth Commandments* is no less convincing. Pastors and educators perform an invaluable service in helping parents fulfill their "mission" to educate their children.

As the Second Vatican Council noted, in this mission parents "should realize that they are thereby cooperating with the love of God the Creator and are, in a certain sense, its interpreters" (*Gaudium et Spes*, 50).

We hope that this curriculum, especially this booklet, will help you interpret human sexuality in its full dignity and beauty, the gift of a loving God.

Nothing we can write in a booklet will *make* your child chaste.

Your honest example, proper teaching, and the power of the sacraments are most crucial in helping children remain chaste.

Chastity is a natural virtue. It is part of the cardinal virtue of Temperance. The holiness of Chastity was recognized by cultures long before the time of Christ. Chastity is also one of the Fruits of the Holy Spirit. This means that there are two ways of looking at Chastity. It is "natural." That is to say, we should not fear that expecting Chastity of a person is excessive. Secondly, Chastity means more than merely avoiding impurity.†

At the same time, as a Fruit of the Holy Spirit, Chastity is the beautiful flowering of an inner grace. As the *Catechism of the Catholic Church* says, "Chastity means the successful integration of sexuality within the person and thus the inner unity of man in his bodily and spiritual being" (CCC: 2337). It is "a gift from God, a *grace*, a fruit of spiritual effort" (CCC: 2345).

Let us not underestimate the "effort" involved. The *Catechism* also notes that "Self-mastery is a *long and exacting work*. One can never consider it acquired once and for all" (cf. CCC: 2342).

This effort is not solely an individual responsibility.

> It also involves a *cultural effort*, for there is "an interdependence between personal betterment and the improvement of society." Chastity presupposes respect for the rights of the person, in particular the right to receive information and an education that respect the moral and spiritual dimensions of human life (CCC: 2344).

* See CCC: Articles 6 and 9 of Part 3 (2331-2400; 2514-2533).

In the Catholic ordering of the Ten Commandments, the sixth and ninth commandments refer to sins against the marriage bond, specifically adultery, fornication, lust, and unnatural forms of birth control.

† "Nevertheless, the Lord's Redemption has made the positive practice of chastity into something that is really possible and a motive for joy, both for those who have the vocation to marriage (before, in the time of preparation, and afterwards, in the course of married life) as well as for those who have the gift of a special calling to the consecrated life.... So chastity is not be be understood as a repressive attitude" (*The Truth and Meaning of Human Sexuality*, §§3, 4).

IT IS OUR HOPE that nothing we have included in *The New Corinthians* curriculum, and especially in this booklet, fails to respect the moral and spiritual dimensions of human life. **If you deem anything presented here to be inappropriate,* your decision is final in the matter.** We hope that we are able to provide a resource for educating your child in Chastity.

* That is, if you deem anything to be too much, too soon.

Without the aid of the Holy Spirit, as St. Paul testifies, it is impossible to be chaste. When it comes to chastity, his observations are very sensible advice for parents as well as adolescents:

> Therefore let any one who thinks that he stands take heed lest he fall. No temptation has overtaken you that is not common to man. God is faithful, and he will not let you be tempted beyond your strength, but with the temptation will also provide the way of escape, that you may be able to endure it (1 Corinthians 10:12-13).

How Do You Tell When to Give This Information?

It is difficult to predict when a girl will enter puberty. For general purposes, the earliest age is usually given as 9, but some girls might not enter it until 14 or even 15. Another rule of thumb is that a girl's first period will occur when her weight reaches between 95 and 105 pounds. This depends on the girl's build and the amount of body fat she carries.

It would be best to establish a continual dialogue with the child from an early age, answering questions as simply as possible when they arise. For a girl of six who asks where babies come from, it is enough to explain, "The baby lives in a special place beneath mom's tummy." At such an age the child's curiosity is easily satisfied.*

* A ten-year-old asked, "What is rape?" Her Mom responded that "It is a violent act against a woman." The girl said, "Oh," ending the conversion.

For a girl approaching puberty the situation is different. She should be prepared before her first menstrual period, though for some girls that may be the first noticeable sign of puberty. For others, the appearance of pubic hair may prompt her to ask you what is happening.

For many, the first sign of puberty will be a change in personality. Anecdotal experience suggests that parents may notice these changes three to six months before such girls show physical signs of puberty. Many girls will become sullen, easily bored, feisty, or irritable as new hormones enter the system. Some parents note that it seems as though the girl has "lost her innocence." She becomes critical of everything; despairing, or untypically assertive in her behavior.

It may be possible to start a mother-daughter conversation that treats some of the topics of puberty. It is certainly not necessary to plow through all the subjects below immediately upon suspicion that the girl is entering puberty. It is often best handled by a continuing dialogue throughout her adolescence.

Topics for Girls

The following information is not meant to be read to nor by *your daughter. It is merely a suggested way for you to convey the information, a way of opening a dialogue with your child. Perhaps you have already communicated some of these points. Many sections concern subjects you may decide your child is not ready to hear about nor will need until later in your mutual dialogue. This dialogue should not be confined to one "talk" but should extend throughout the child's adolescence and into adulthood.*

"There's Something I'd Like to Tell You..."

SOON YOU WILL BE GOING THROUGH CHANGES as your body prepares to be an adult. I'd like to be the one to introduce you to this part of your life. I want you to know that I'll be here for you as you go through these changes and I want you to feel comfortable talking with me about these things.

The first thing I want you to know is that God made you. He made you a woman and your fertility gives you the possibility of co-creating another human being. This is a great privilege. It is also a great responsibility.

God also intended that the love between husband and wife be joyful. The marital embrace was meant by God to be a sign of the commitment that husband and wife make when they marry. If you don't remember anything else, remember this: In God's plan, the marital embrace, commonly called sexual intercourse, is exclusively a marriage act. It's supposed to be a symbolic renewal of the marriage covenant between husband and wife. It ought to say, "We take each other for better and worse."

Marriage is a sacrament. It is a channel of God's grace to His People. So, it should be joyfully celebrated, and the marital embrace ought to be a joyous expression of married love.

The Marital Embrace

(You may choose to explain the following section on intercourse in your own words. It is preferred that from early childhood parents gradually introduce the concepts of sperm and egg—separate from treating the subject of intercourse—in explaining reproduction. Familiarity with these terms will prepare the child to understand that the act of intercourse is not to be associated with elimination.)*

*"Another important task for parents is following the gradual physiological development of their daughters and helping them joyfully to accept the development of their femininity in a bodily, psychological and spiritual sense. . . . Therefore, normally, one should discuss the cycles of fertility and their meaning. But it is still *not necessary to give detailed explanations about sexual union, unless this is explicitly requested*" [italics added] (Pontifical Council for the Family, *The Truth and Meaning of Human Sexuality*, §90).

WHAT IS THE MARRIAGE ACT? The marriage act is a physical union of husband and wife in which the husband transmits the seed of human life to his wife. When a man becomes sexually aroused, the circulation system in his penis is made so that blood temporarily cannot escape. This causes the tissue of the penis to become firm, in what is called an *erection*. It becomes impossible for the man to urinate, because that channel is closed by the erection. Another channel opens which carries a fluid called sperm from the man's testicles.

In sexual intercourse the husband places his penis in his wife's vagina. Millions of sperm cells are released when the man ejaculates at the peak moment of his sexual arousal. Each sperm cell has a long tail that it uses to swim through the cervix, into the uterus, and eventually into the wife's Fallopian tubes. This is where it will meet the egg cell and combine to conceive a baby.

God intended sexual intercourse to be fertile, that is, to bring babies into existence. He also intended that intercourse unite husband and wife in love.The marriage act is meant to increase the bond between the spouses and their love for each other. The child that God creates from their marital embrace inherits the love that this act is intended to reflect and strengthen.

It is important to remember that God wants every act of intercourse to serve both of these purposes: to unite the couple in love and to be open—or at least not intentionally closed—to His plan for creating new life.

God has joined these tremendous blessings of Love and Life in the marriage act. The Catholic Church regards intercourse between husband and wife so important that it calls it "the marriage act."[†] What Jesus teaches about marriage applies also to the marriage act: *"What God has joined, let no one take apart*" (Matthew 19:6).

† God intends that sexual intercourse should be exclusively an act between husband and wife. For this reason we use the term "marital embrace," "marital act," or "marriage act" in this booklet.

This act ought to be – at least implicitly – a renewal of the love and commitment that the spouses made at their wedding.

Note: This last sentence holds the fundamental reason for the Church's opposition to many contemporary sexual practices. One the one hand, the body language of contraceptive behavior says, "We take each other for better but definitely *not* for the imagined 'worse' of possible pregnancy." Because this contradicts the marriage covenant, it makes the act invalid as a marriage act and therefore immoral. On the other hand, artificial insemination, test tube reproduction, and surrogate motherhood each fail to include the uniting love of spouses in the act of reproduction. These topics will be treated more fully in high school, but many younger children will have been made familiar with condoms by this age. As soon as a communication has begun with the child concerning sexual intercourse, the reasons for the Church's opposition to these practices should also be communicated briefly and emphatically.

As your body matures and prepares for fertility, you will experience many changes, both physical and emotional. You are not only preparing for the possibility of bearing children, but also of loving a spouse. Both of these things are wonderful gifts from God to married people.

Because your body is becoming capable of bearing children, you may be sensing some of the feelings that go with sexual arousal. They are new to you and may be powerful and frightening. They are not evil feelings, but the result of natural forces in your body that prepare you to express your love for a future spouse in sexual intimacy.

Not everyone marries. You may feel called to the religious life, or to a life of dedicated singleness. This does not mean that your fertility and your sexuality are useless. You were created a sexual being—a woman—for a reason.

People who live celibate lives offer their sexuality as a total gift of themselves to God. Their sexuality is not expressed through marital intercourse, but that does not mean they turn off their sexuality, or are emotionally deprived. God brightens their lives with emotional and spiritual delights just as He does married people, but in a different way.

In any case, as your body matures over the next few years, you will experience physical and emotional changes that I want to help prepare you for now.

The Gift of Fertility

THE FIRST CHANGES YOU NOTICE on entering puberty are the development of breast tissue and the cyclical bleeding pattern called *menstruation*. Your hips will begin to broaden to make room for a possible pregnancy. Your breasts will develop, including the glands that will produce milk once a baby is born (which will be discussed later). These changes are produced by hormones now circulating in your blood. Let's look at menstruation first.

Ovulation and Menstruation

The *menstrual cycle* involved here results from the regular ripening of one or two eggs in your ovaries and the preparation of your uterus, or womb, to carry a baby.

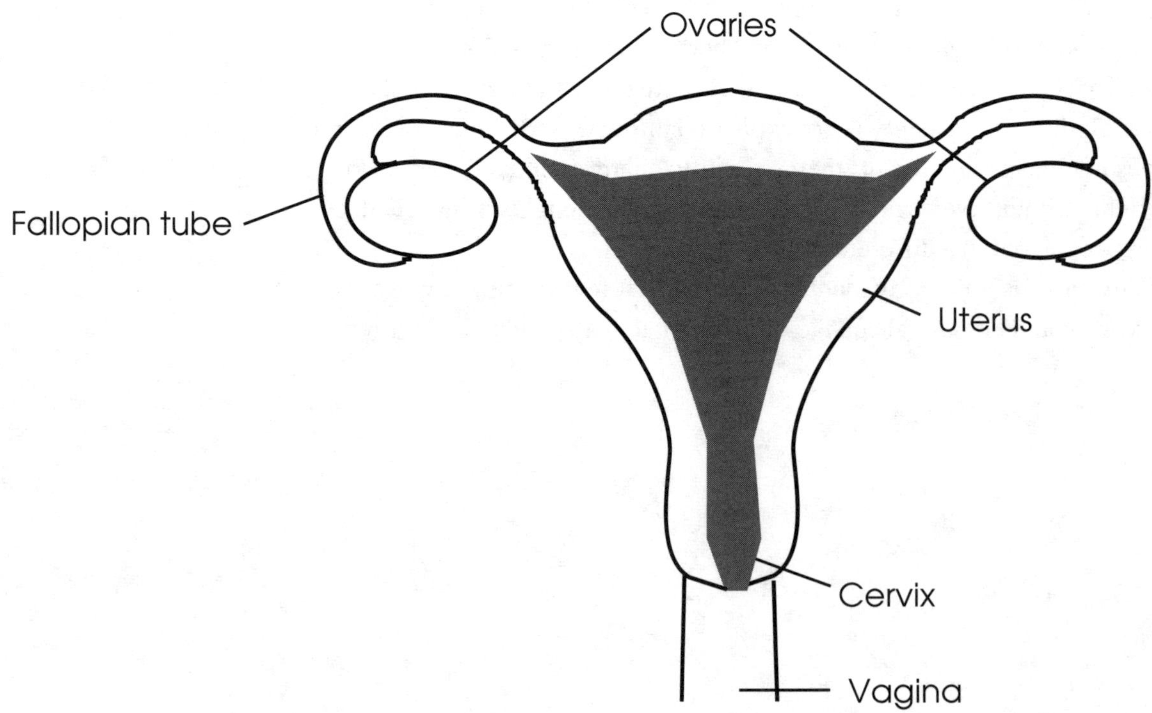

The *ovaries* are located on either side of your *uterus* in the lower part of your abdomen. Each ovary is about the size of an almond. They contain thousands of eggs, each of which contains one half of the chromosomes (genetic material) needed to create a baby.

Between each ovary and the uterus is a tube (Fallopian tube) through which the egg moves.

The pituitary gland is the master gland of your body. It directs everything that goes on. It is the size of a pea and is located at the base of your brain. At the beginning of a menstrual cycle, your pituitary gland tells the ovaries to prepare one or two eggs for release. During this ripening process, the ovaries secrete a hormone called estrogen that causes changes to make you more fertile, more capable of becoming pregnant.

THE MENSTRUAL CYCLE usually takes around 28-30 days, from the first day of bleeding in one cycle through the last day before the next period. It is not unusual to have a 25 day cycle, or a 35 day cycle. Some women always have cycles longer than 30 days. If a woman's cycle varies more than two weeks from her shortest one to her longest one, she is said to have "irregular cycles," and there might be a physical problem. Often better nutrition or the woman's first pregnancy will make her future menstrual cycles more regular, but this may not always be the case.

The release of the egg into the tube is called *ovulation*. After ovulation the ovaries signal the pituitary gland to stop any further eggs from being released. At this stage of the menstrual cycle, a new hormone takes over. It is called progesterone and it controls the woman's fertility for about two weeks.

One of progesterone's effects is to keep the lining of the uterus rich with blood to sustain a newly conceived life. If a pregnancy hasn't occurred, however, the production of progesterone will cease after a couple of weeks. The lining of the uterus is sloughed off in what is commonly known as your "period," and your next menstrual cycle begins with the first day of bleeding or spotting.

Let's back up a second.

During the process of ovulation, the hormone estrogen causes a change in your body that confuses some girls. Estrogen makes glands in your cervix (located at the opening to the uterus) produce a mucus discharge. Sometimes it makes you feel "wet" outside the vagina; sometimes you will notice it on the tissue paper when you wipe after urination. This is a normal, healthy secretion and an important part of your fertility.

This *cervical mucus* does a number of things: It provides a *swimming medium for sperm,* which is the male contribution to the process of reproduction; and it provides the perfect *nutrition* for the sperm cell.

Conception

I mentioned the Fallopian tubes and the sperm cells earlier. If the egg released at ovulation meets sperm cells in the Fallopian tube, they will surround it. One sperm cell will be admitted into the egg to cause conception. All the others are excluded a split second after that one cell penetrates the egg's lining. *At this time an immortal soul is created by God.* That means the soul will live forever regardless of what happens to the new life.

The 23 chromosomes* of the sperm cell will unite with the 23 chromosomes in the *nucleus* of the egg and at that moment a unique human being is conceived. Once conception occurs, it will take several days to move through the tube and nest, or *implant*, in the womb. Baby then draws nourishment from the mother's blood supply during pregnancy.

*Chromosomes hold the genes that determine all our characteristics: our height, hair color, eye color, bone thickness, eyesight, and a million other things that make you a unique creation of God.

Our fertility "is a good, a gift and an end of marriage. By giving life, spouses participate in God's fatherhood" (CCC: 2398).

Pregnancy and Childbirth

Within three weeks the child's heart is beating and pumping its own blood. At one month, all the fingers and toes are present, complete with prints that will be unique to that person. By the 40th day after conception, brain waves can be detected. It is true that a woman does not feel her baby move until the fourth or fifth month (when the child is about a foot long), but the baby responds to touch and light at eight weeks. By that time, all the baby's vital organs have been formed, the systems that will function throughout the rest of his or her life.

At the end of the pregnancy, the baby will send out a hormone that tells the mother's body that it is time to deliver her baby. She will go into labor and give birth. Her breasts will then provide milk for the child's nourishment. *Prolactin*, a hormone produced by breastfeeding, helps bond the mother psychologically to her infant.

For a long time people believed that babies couldn't see at birth. In reality, they have a limited ability to see soon after they are born. However, the baby's eyes can focus only for a short distance—the distance from mother's elbow to her face. God has designed things in such a way that the baby's first view of the world will be the image of its loving mother's face.

Natural Family Planning in Christian Marriage

The appearance of cervical mucus and other bodily changes can be noted and used by married couples in *Natural Family Planning*, or NFP. This is a moral way by which spouses decide whether to have marital relations or not depending on the needs of their family.

The Church approves of Natural Family Planning. It does not separate what God has joined in sexual intercourse: love and life. The spouses simply postpone intercourse when they have serious reasons to postpone a pregnancy. They give up sexual relations to regulate the size of their family.

Modern NFP is highly effective.* It differs from the Rhythm Method in that it follows your personal cycle. Artificial contraception, sterilization, or direct abortion are never moral—*they are never necessary.*† Natural Family Planning is a gift of God to our times, a way for Christians to remain chaste throughout married life.

Let me summarize all this. The menstrual cycle is all about preparing an egg for possible fertilization. It is a complex process with many mysteries yet to be understood. Your fertility is a delicate mechanism. Take care of it. Immoral forms of birth control can permanently damage the balance of hormones, scar the delicate Fallopian Tubes, and make the womb incapable of sustaining a future, desired pregnancy. It is not only wrong to separate what God intended to be joined in the act of intercourse, it is wrong to subject the gift of your fertility to harm.

We may never sin in order to achieve even the best results. Neither may we risk our fertility, the precious ability to bring forth new life, for our own convenience. Fortunately, Natural Family Planning (NFP) is medically safe and very effective, and there is never any need for such a risk.

Before marriage a couple should receive full instruction on NFP. Here, I want to merely stress that this is an effective and morally acceptable practice. There is no reason for a Catholic woman to disregard her Church's teaching concerning birth control.

NFP is respectful towards God's gift of fertility. Couples who practice it find that it encourages respect between husband and wife. Good things are worth waiting for and *sexual intercourse is a good thing.* Immoral birth control places the pleasure of intercourse above the gift of fertility. In contraceptive sex, the body language of the couple says, "We take each other for 'better' but very definitely not for the imagined 'worse' of possible pregnancy." In that way they oppose the marital meaning of sex as a renewal of their marriage covenant. If a husband insists on contraceptive sex, he's telling his wife, "I take you for the pleasures of sex, but leave your fertility behind."

Your fertility is not something to be tossed aside as if it doesn't matter. Never let sexual feelings, romantic illusions, or pressure from others lead you to misuse God's wonderful gifts of fertility and procreation.

* Studies of the Sympto-Thermal Method have found it to be as effective as the Pill. Studies commonly show that this form of Natural Family Planning is capable of achieving a 99% effectiveness. For more information on Natural Family Planning, contact The Couple to Couple League, P.O. Box 111184, Cincinnati, OH 45211.

† See **Artificial Birth Control & Abortion** on p. 27. These practices are "objectively evil acts," which are defined on p. 320 of the curriculum.

The use of hormonal medications in the control of specific gynecological pathologies is not the same as artificial birth control. Similarly, indirect abortion resulting from other efforts to save the life of the mother is not the same as direct abortion (cf. CCC:2271).

The Breast

About a year before the beginning of periods, called *menarche*, girls begin forming breast tissue. It is one of the first signs of the onset of puberty. The whole breast enlarges and the nipple and the area that surround it, known as the areola, will change as well. The areola, with the nipple in the center, stands out from the flesh around it and develops a delicate pinkish color. Sometimes one breast will grow faster than the other, but this is normal.

When the breasts enlarge, they can be quite tender, particularly in the nipple region. During the week before menstruation this can be very noticeable. This tenderness may even begin before you start having periods.

When the breasts start developing it is important to dress modestly in order not to draw attention to them, and to prevent embarrassing accidents. A brassiere will prevent much of the discomfort from tenderness and the "floppy" feeling you may experience during exercise. It is important not to try to hide your breasts either, by adopting a round-shouldered posture. Whatever your eventual development, your figure is always improved by carrying yourself in a proper posture.

Dressing with modesty is the best way to avoid drawing undue and disrespectful attention.*

* **Modesty**—The Fruit of the Holy Spirit by which we reflect in our external actions strive to avoid provoking the lustful desire condemned by Jesus in Matthew 5:28. As the Catechism states: "Modesty protects the mystery of persons and their love" (CCC: 2522).

In practice, dressing with modesty means using loose-fitting and non-revealing clothing over your breasts; it also means wearing loose-fitting and sufficiently long clothing that does not draw attention to your genital area.

The breast serves an important function in the care of babies. It provides nourishment. The best nutrition a baby can get is the milk provided by the mother. The best claim a manufacturer of baby formula can make is that his product is "almost as good as breast milk."

Even if baby formula provided the same nourishment, there is another function served by breastfeeding. Antibodies to germs are manufactured at the nipple and given to the baby during feeding. This is one reason why breastfed babies enjoy better health. The breast provides the protection needed right now to fight those diseases to which an infant may be exposed.

In the process of breastfeeding, a hormone called *prolactin* is produced. This hormone has been called the "mothering hormone," since it produces feelings of comfort and relaxation in the mother. This helps her to bond with her baby.

Hormones affect more than just physical changes, as you will discover throughout your life as a woman. Research is showing that breastfeeding is a possible preventive measure against breast cancer, but that is trivial compared to the good that breastfeeding does by creating a bond of love between a mother and her baby.

I realize you might know or have heard of mothers who were unable to breastfeed for one reason or another. *I'm not saying that women who don't nurse can't be good mothers or raise healthy children.* The point of all this is to provide you with a proper appreciation of why God gave you breasts in the first place.

Nature's Method of Spacing Babies

It should be mentioned briefly that, in most cases, the hormone prolactin, produced by the suckling of the baby, *suppresses ovulation.* The amount of suckling needed to suppress ovulation varies from mother to mother. Most women who nurse on demand, not using bottles, formula, pacifiers, etc., will average between nine and twenty months after childbirth before the return of fertility.*

Breastfeeding can be a natural way to space babies between 18 and 24 months apart. Some mothers are unable to breastfeed for medical reasons, but they may achieve a natural spacing as well by using NFP.

* This form of mothering is called "Ecological Breastfeeding" and differs significantly from the way breastfeeding is ordinarily done in American culture. The rules for following this form of natural child-spacing cannot be treated fully in this space. It is introduced here in order to convey an understanding of the relationship between nursing and fertility. For a thorough treatment of the subject, see Sheila Kippley's *Breastfeeding and Natural Child-Spacing* and *The Art of Natural Family Planning,* by John and Sheila Kippley. Both books available from The Couple to Couple League: 1-800-745-8252.

Health and Hygiene

NOW IS THE TIME to develop good habits of hygiene and nutrition that will serve you the rest of your life. A girl begins undergoing changes in her weight and height beginning around age 10.

The fastest growth takes place around 12.

As you pass into puberty you will need to use feminine napkins during your period. Change napkins frequently during the first few days of heavy menstrual bleeding. This prevents unpleasant odors and protects your clothes from seepage.

Public women's restrooms have a special container for placing the used napkin when you change. If there isn't a drawer or bin for them, use the wastepaper basket. Never flush a sanitary napkin down the toilet, since it will block up the plumbing.

You should take a warm bath daily during your period. It will do a lot to make you feel fresher. Enjoy any games or sports you normally do, but you might want to cut out swimming during the first days of heavy flow. It's not unusual to be a little constipated during menstruation. Make sure you get plenty of fresh fruit and vegetables. You'll also need more rest for the first couple of nights during your period.

Problems with Menstruation

If your bleeding is excessive you must tell me. If your periods occur more frequently than once every three weeks, or if you use more than a dozen napkins per period, it is excessive. You may become anemic, an illness that results from losing too much blood. (Note: Most girls who experience heavy menstrual bleeding between ages 12 and 15 get over it naturally, and some find relief through dietary supplements. Anecdotal evidence indicates that capsicum, i.e., cayenne pepper, and chlorophyll* can be helpful for many.) Be sure to get enough iron in your diet to prevent anemia.

During your period you will probably feel a "dragging" sensation in your lower abdomen. Some girls experience a certain amount of cramping during their menstrual flow. There can be some sharp pains as well, but this is normal. If you get regular exercise but don't exhaust yourself, you have fewer tendencies to suffer pain during menstruation. The anemia and constipation we discussed often contribute to this pain as well.

One gram (1000 mg.) of magnesium alleviates cramping for many girls and women within two or three hours. If that doesn't work, we can try aspirin, Tylenol, Midol, or any number of other over-the-counter medications.

Painful menstruation, like heavy menstrual bleeding, may be treatable by natural means. There are nutritional ways that may reduce and even eliminate menstrual cramps. Marilyn Shannon's book, *Fertility, Cycles and Nutrition,*† is full of valuable information and insights into the relationship between food and reproductive health.

If you still have cramps, you may want to start making a note of how long you go from one period to the next. If you have a fairly regular cycle, you can begin to predict when you will suffer your next bout with cramps. It then might help to make sure you are getting enough magnesium in your diet throughout your cycle. Calcium, zinc, and vitamin D are also important to watch.

Also, having a record of how long your cycles are will help when you learn Natural Family Planning. The more information you have about your own cycles, the easier it will be to use NFP when you are married.

* Chlorophyll is available in either liquid or tablet form. It may be taken shortly before or during menstruation (60 mg/day or that amount taken after each meal as needed).

Calcium is necessary to the clotting process as well. Magnesium is needed to help the body use calcium, and vitamin D is important in calcium absorption.

† See Marilyn Shannon, *Fertility, Cycles and Nutrition*, pp. 77-80. This book is available from The Couple to Couple League, P.O. Box 111184, Cincinnati, OH 45211, $10.95 plus shipping and handling. **Order toll free:** 1-800-745-8252.

The Bitter Pill

Many young women are given artificial hormones, the birth control Pill, when they go to a physician complaining of menstrual cramps or irregular cycles. Both are common experiences and seldom due to any disease.

The full side effects of the Pill are just barely becoming known today, and those effects are even greater on girls who are just beginning their fertile years. The Pill is dangerous to your health and to your future fertility. Many women also note that menstrual problems disappear with age and especially with the birth of their first child.

The birth control Pill is an *abortifacient*. This means that it can cause a newly conceived child to be aborted. The Pill does not always prevent ovulation. It will make conditions less favorable for pregnancy.* No Pill, however, is 100 percent effective.

If a pregnancy occurs, the Pill threatens the newly conceived life by making the lining of the uterus hostile to implantation. When the cycle of Pills brings on the next menstrual period, the baby is "sloughed off." This is a *chemically caused abortion.*[†]

Most women do not know this, and the medical establishment does little to educate women about how the Pill works.

The Pill really doesn't make "regular" menstrual cycles. It causes symptoms that imitate a menstrual cycle. Periods occur at a certain time due to artificial hormones and not those made by the ovulation process. Women on the Pill think they are having "regular" cycles, but these hormones are capable of causing regular bleeding episodes even in an elderly woman.

It may seem that using the Pill for birth control and using NFP are no different because they have the same goal.[‡] Not so. Earning money to buy something and breaking a shop window to steal it also have the same goal. One way of attaining that goal, however, breaks the Seventh Commandment. Deliberately making the body infertile to prevent pregnancy is an immoral means of birth control. Each act of intercourse is meant to be open to God's plan for creating human life, according to the mutual fertility of the husband and wife.

We are caretakers of our fertility, not owners. A caretaker may only use something the way its owner wants it used. If someone loans you their house while they are away, you don't have the right to take off the roof just because the living room is too dark during the day.

* The hormones of the Pill do this by reducing the quantity and changing the quality of the cervical mucus. Sperm have a more difficult time reaching the place of conception.

† Another abortifacient, the intrauterine device (IUD), works primarily by causing early abortions. For more information, see "The Pill and the IUD" and "The Pill: How It Works," available from The Couple to Couple League, P.O. Box 111184, Cincinnati, OH 45211.

‡ See also *Marriage Is for Keeps,* chapter 8, and *The Art of Natural Family Planning*, chapter 19.

Other Concerns

Menstruation isn't the only discharge associated with fertility. When estrogen is preparing for ovulation, mucus usually starts appearing at the opening of the vagina. It is important to wash daily and perhaps use a sanitary napkin at the height of the mucus discharge during the fertile time of the cycle. One of the changes of puberty will be the growth of pubic hair around the genital region, under the arms, and on the legs. The hormones can produce unpleasant odors, so you'll want to use an underarm deodorant at this time.

The changes in your body's chemistry can also produce a change in the makeup of the oils (sebum) that lubricate your skin. For a while it becomes more difficult for those oils to reach the surface layer and exit the openings, or pores, of the skin. This blockage makes a good environment for the bacteria that are normally found on the surface of the skin. A pimple forms.

This condition is called acne and it is part of going through puberty. If you handle or squeeze the pimples, you risk spreading the bacteria in high concentrations to other pores. Infection can worsen along with discoloration. Scabs form to protect and aid in healing the damaged skin. If these are picked as well, scar tissue may form.

The best treatment for acne is to wash your face once or twice a day with a skin cleanser. Be sure to drink enough water, which helps keep skin healthy.

Acne usually goes away by the late teens or early twenties.

Nutrition, Fat, and Fertility

Eating well is vital not only to your health—including your fertility—but to your mental attitude. Many girls in our society are unhappy with their bodies and blame it on food. So much stress is placed on how we look, and girls can be misled into believing their problems will all go away if they just get skinny enough. The standards of beauty have been cruel to women over the last 30 years.

Since the mid-1960s, models and the fashions they wear have forced women into accepting a standard of beauty that is hazardous for their fertility. Our secular culture has accepted an idea that the marriage act is "for fun only." This demeans our sexuality. It makes women into toys for men, not their beloved companions for life.

A certain ratio of body fat (20-22%) is absolutely necessary to your fertility and to your overall health. Estrogen is stored in the extra layer of fat God has designed into the make-up of a woman. The body uses this estrogen for fertility, but it also has other functions, such as building strong bones.

A girl who starves herself to look good may be opening herself up to *osteoporosis*, a disease in which bones break easily. This disease is becoming more common in American women today. It was once unheard of in women younger than premenopause. (Premenopause is the time of life immediately before a woman stops ovulating.)

There is nothing wrong with healthy, vigorous physical exercise. However, if exercise takes off too much body fat, your periods may become infrequent and more painful.

A woman who is at her proper weight will have relatively more pounds of body fat than a man at his proper weight. You may not think that's fair, but that's how God designed the female body. Don't destroy your health trying to look like a skeleton.

Rest and Relaxation

Regular sleep is important now. Establishing good sleeping habits takes discipline, but it's a discipline that will serve you well throughout life. This is important to your mental as well as physical health. If you starve your body just to look slim and stay up too late studying or socializing, you risk your physical health – particularly your fertility, your appearance, and also your mental well-being.

Our emotions depend a great deal on a proper balance of nutrients in our bodies. We also need rest and relaxation to refresh our spirits. As the body needs rest to repair itself from the day's wear and tear, the mind needs relaxation to recover from the day's stress.

Give yourself the best chances to be happy and healthy by getting at least seven hours of uninterrupted sleep each night. Schedule time to relax with a good book, pursue a hobby, or socialize with friends. The coming of adulthood brings many changes into your life. One of them is stress. The work of childhood is play. Adulthood can become so busy and demanding that you forget that your mind, as well as your body, needs play. If you participate in competitive sports, you may be getting great exercise, but the stress of competing can rob you of the relaxation you need.

Relaxation protects your spirit from the constant pressure of stress in your life. It allows you to "wake up and smell the roses." Attending Mass and other prayer devotions will also help break the grip of stress, allowing you to focus on heaven.

It's not unusual to find it more difficult to sleep due to the many stresses in your life right now. Caffeine or snacks eaten before bed may keep you up, so it is good to see if cutting these out will help. If you get a good amount of exercise during the day, it will also help make sleep come more easily. If worries are causing you to lie awake, it is important to talk things over. You can talk to me. Trust in God, pray the Rosary and ask Our Lady to help you get the rest you need to face tomorrow's events.

Emotional Changes

PUBERTY often brings on a time of turmoil in young people. The effects of the fertility hormones in your system can cause mood swings. You may find yourself irritated or depressed for no apparent reason. It is good that this happens. Learning to handle the stresses and emotions of life is part of growing up. We don't always understand immediately what is happening to us, and we have to learn to ask our feelings what they are trying to tell us. We have to be able to apply the reason God gave us to make good judgments about situations and choices.*

* "In themselves passions are neither good nor evil. They are morally qualified only to the extent that they effectively engage reason and will.... Passions are morally good when they contribute to a good action, evil in the opposite case" (CCC: 1767-1768).

You are also becoming independent, no longer a child. On the one hand, you want to be more responsible for your life. You yearn to show the world what you can do on your own. On the other hand, it is normal to fear the unknown. The future will bring sorrows as well as joys. Decisions you make now will influence the rest of your life in ways you may not like. You don't want to be cowardly, but you don't want to be rash either. This causes anxiety, which is a nervous feeling before the uncertain future.

Alcohol and Drugs

Some young people try to cover up the painful feelings that come during this time. Alcohol, nicotine, and worse drugs can smother your normal feelings. They have that effect for a while, but when the feelings return, the mind and body crave another dose. As the use of these continues, the amount of the dose needed increases. The whole process snowballs into either physical or psychological addiction. Your freedom to live without these things becomes lost. They become one more problem in your life.

In the meantime, you haven't dealt with any of the real causes of the feelings that drugs and alcohol suppress. Your feelings are there to provoke you, to make you act. The burning sensation when you put your hand on a frying pan is there to tell you that the pan is hot. The pain makes you pull your hand away.

If you were drugged, however, you might not feel the pain, or your reflexes might be slowed. You would get seriously burned.

I want you to tell me how you are feeling. Don't be ashamed of your feelings. If you're angry, for example, it is difficult to talk to people. You don't reason very well under the influence of anger. That doesn't mean you should be embarrassed for having that feeling.

If you allow your anger to build up unreasonably, that is wrong.

One of the best ways to prevent that from happening is to realize when you are angry and immediately try to understand and resolve what is making you feel that way.

This is all part of learning how to be an adult. If a man throws a temper tantrum every time something goes wrong, it is considered childish. If his anger is reasonable, that is another matter. Say his anger is caused by another person's injustice towards him. It is a sign of maturity if he can talk with that person confidently and try to work things out between them. It is childish to harbor a grudge or sneak around trying to "get even."

Your emotions are there for a reason. Anger is meant to energize your will to attack whatever threatens you. Fear motivates you to flee.

Since physically fighting or fleeing our problems isn't often acceptable, we end up having to swallow our emotions. We end up depressed, like animals in cages unable to exert our wills.

Alcohol and many other drugs can be used as anesthetics—to kill pain. It isn't hard to see how tempting this could be to someone who is going through the emotions of adolescence.

Emotions can be frightening and painful. Drugs can mask them, turn them around, or even turn them off. They can provide a temporary feeling of well-being, a fantasy not based in reality.

The tragedy of drugs is that they give a false sense of hope. When things bother us, we should take our concerns to Jesus in prayer. He is our hope and His Truth sets us free. When we look for a quick solution in drugs, we buy into a lie.

Drugs can produce psychological addiction. Some people even become *psychologically* addicted to eating as a way of relieving stress and getting a temporary good feeling. The so-called "legal drugs," alcohol and nicotine, also cause a *physical* addiction in a relatively short time. Illegal drugs are usually much more addictive and have profound effects on a person's moods. "Crack" cocaine is so addictive that even a single use may be addictive.

The addict finds that he is unable to stop abusing his body because his happiness rests so completely on the lie he has accepted.

There are proper uses for many substances, but none for the addictive illegal drugs. The rule for food and drink is to use them in moderation. This is the virtue of temperance.

The Catechism states:

> The virtue of temperance disposes us *to avoid every kind of excess*: the abuse of food, alcohol, tobacco, or medicine. Those incur grave guilt who, by drunkenness or a love of speed, endanger their own and others' safety on the road, at sea, or in the air.
>
> The *use of drugs* inflicts very grave damage on human health and life. Their use, except on strictly therapeutic grounds, is a grave offense. Clandestine [secretive] production of and trafficking in drugs are scandalous practices. They constitute direct co-operation in evil, since they encourage people to practices gravely contrary to the moral law (CCC: 2290-2291).

Many people in our culture make light of drug use. They glamorize the "fast life" of wild parties, reckless driving, and irresponsible actions. They do not tell you about the pain and cost of trading the hope of heaven for the lie of "getting high." It is a depressing thing, and the reason they use drugs in the first place is to avoid depression. Don't be fooled. There can be no lasting joy when it involves offending God. Place your trust in Him: "For the Lord will be your confidence and will keep your foot from being caught" (Proverbs 3:26).

Masturbation and Homosexuality

Note: This is a delicate topic and should be discussed only after you discern that your daughter has achieved a reasonable level of maturity. "Homosexuality should not be discussed before adolescence unless a specific serious problem has arisen in a particular situation" (*The Truth and Meaning of Human Sexuality*, §125b).

Because I love you I must warn you against another temptation that comes during times of great stress in life. Sexual feelings can be used just like a drug. They can be generated by the act called masturbation (or self-stimulation) as well as by intercourse. But this is wrong. Any stimulation of the sexual organs outside marriage is immoral, and masturbation totally separates love from life.

The Church has always taught that seeking sexual pleasure for itself is lust, a capital sin (CCC: 2351). We are never to use our own bodies or another person's merely to satisfy lust. The wonderful feelings of our sexuality are intended to make us love a husband more deeply. Masturbation, like sex outside marriage, cannot do this; it is a serious* sin (CCC: 2352). It is a bad habit to start and difficult one to break.

* See p. 229 of the curriculum on examining conscience. Also see p. 315.

At times when you are angry, feel bad about yourself, lonely, or bored, the temptation may arise to masturbate. It never helps anything, but only makes you feel worse. The struggle in life is to love others, and masturbation takes away the drive that would send our love outside ourselves to others. If you are ever tempted to masturbate, resist it with all your might. Pray for help and change your situation immediately so that you don't entertain the temptation.

Two people of the same sex cannot have sexual intercourse that is open to life.* Some men are attracted to men, some women to women. There are numerous theories about why this happens, but the sexual acts they perform are contrary to nature and offensive to God (CCC: 2357). Some in our society see no difference between these homosexual acts and married, or heterosexual, love. They believe that if two homosexuals feel love for each other, the nature of their sexual intercourse doesn't matter.

We believe the Church has received her teaching on sexual love directly from God, Who is Love. The Church cannot be wrong, but she is often misunderstood. Homosexual acts are sins contrary to nature. In the Scriptures, the sin of sodomy is condemned as one of the "sins that cry to Heaven."†

Sodomy is generally defined as any unnatural sexual relations. More specifically, it is any sexual relations between two males.‡ With homosexuals, there is no possibility of their relations resulting in life. They are by nature closed to life.

The Church urges that homosexuals be "accepted with respect, compassion, and sensitivity. Every sign of unjust discrimination in their regard should be avoided" (CCC: 2358).

Homosexuals are called to embrace the same life of chastity expected of all followers of Christ. (See CCC: 2359.) This is difficult, but we are not to make it even more difficult by hatred. This will only have the effect of turning them away from the Truth, who alone can set them free from their sin.

We hate the sin, never the sinner.

Homosexual persons are called to chastity. By the virtues of self-mastery that teach them inner freedom, at times by the support of disinterested friendship, by prayer and sacramental grace, they can and should gradually and resolutely approach Christian perfection.

— CCC: 2359

* "Basing itself on Sacred Scripture, which presents homosexual acts as acts of grave depravity, tradition has always declared that 'homosexual acts are intrinsically disordered.' They are contrary to the natural law. They close the sexual act to the gift of life. They do not proceed from a genuine affective and sexual complementarity. Under no circumstances can they be approved" (CCC: 2357).

† See CCC: 1867.
The other sins that cry to heaven for punishment are willful murder, oppression of the poor, widows and orphans, and defrauding laborers.

‡Rejection of the sin of sodomy is not just a "Catholic" matter. Contraception was unanimously condemned by all Christian denominations as a form of marital sodomy, the sin of Onan (see Genesis 38:8-10). This unanimity held until 1930 when the Anglican Bishops at the Council of Lambeth approved use of some forms of contraception for married couples in difficult situations. For more information on the traditional Protestant view, read *The Bible and Birth Control* by Charles Provan, available from The Couple to Couple League, 1-800-745-8252.

The Other Half

It has not been considered necessary to present any graphic of the male anatomy for this section since diagrams of external sexual organs, however abstract, may produce unnecessary curiosity and contribute little to the discussion of the "facts of life."

The female internal organs were diagrammed in order to aid the discussion of when and where life begins.

FEMALE FERTILITY comes and goes in a cycle. Men, however, are fertile all the time. God made male fertility this way to increase the chances that sexual intercourse would result in new life.

Puberty for boys is slightly later than it is for girls. Usually between the ages of 11 and 13 a boy will undergo a change due to the hormone testosterone. This hormone causes the male body to produce the sperm cells that are released during the marital embrace. Each cell contains one half of the chromosomes (genetic material) needed to create a baby.

Along with the production of sperm cells, testosterone has other effects on men. It causes their emotions to be less stable, more excitable. In addition, the hormone creates in men a natural urge for sexual intimacy. This is controllable, but there is no denying that a boy's sexual attraction can be stimulated quite easily by the way women around him dress and act.

Male sexual attraction is mainly stimulated by sight and by thoughts of physical intimacy. The sexual feelings and interests of girls focus more on emotional and social involvements. When two young people of the opposite sex look at each other, the chances are slim that they are thinking about the same thing. The girl may be thinking about forming a new relationship, dating, and having pleasant time. The boy may think of all these things, but with the added fantasy of a sexual relationship. If encouraged or allowed by the girl, the boy may be tempted to the sin of fornication, that is, intercourse between unmarried people.

As if to protect women, who bear the children that may be conceived from such acts, young girls mature in their sexual development* before boys

* The difference in male and female sex drives was described well by John Quesnell:

> When a young man is capable of having erections and ejaculating semen, he develps sexual desire. At about age sixteen, he has a fully developed sexual drive. He wants to see a girl's nude body, to caress her body, and to have intercourse with her. It is a full drive and the sex drive is mature.
>
> A young woman wants a young man, but she does not have a desire to see his naked body, to fondle him, or to have orgasm. She wants a man, but not in that way. She wants him to hold her, she wants him to want her, she wants him to say she is beautiful and that he loves her. She wants love. Her drive for love becomes mature at sixteen or seventeen. Although a woman matures physically before a man and although she can conceive and have a child at a younger age than he can father a child, her drive for sexual orgasm is immature. She is curious, but her drive for orgasm and sexual intimacy is not in the same ball park as that of the man (*Holy Terrors and Holy Parents*, Franciscan Herald Press, Chicago, 1975, p. 157).

do. Girls will usually have their first period one or two years before a boy the same age enters puberty. Young girls should be protected from older males. They are seldom intimidated by boys their same age.

On the other hand, girls will be attracted to boys a few years older than themselves. Older boys may have become skilled at convincing young girls that they love them. They pretend to give love in order to get sex. Unfortunately, too many girls fall for their lies.

Sex outside marriage not only breaks the commandments, it is *unjust to any child* that may be conceived. No matter what birth control two unwed people use, they risk introducing a third person into their relationship. In today's abortion culture, unwed pregnancy exposes girls to the further temptation to take the life of an unborn child. It is wrong to put yourself in a position where such a risk exists.*

*For more information, consult the section, "Occasions of Sin," on p. 45, which deals with the moral responsibility of Catholics to avoid "near occasions of sin."

The Meaning of Sexuality

YOUR SEXUAL FEELINGS are meant for a good purpose, and so are boys' sexual feelings. They are part of the way God made you as a sexual being. They incline you to love your spouse and nurture a child. Likewise, the male sexual urge inclines him to take on the role of a loving spouse and father. When these feelings occur within the context of marriage, great good arises, not only for the couple and their children, but for society as well. A chaste marriage reflects the great love God has for us. He wants our sexuality to be for us a preview of the complete joy of heaven.

Being chaste does not mean denying our sexuality. It means understanding and desiring God's plan for our sexuality, which is to generate love. With that understanding and desire come self-mastery. The Catechism explains it:

> Charity is the *form* of all the virtues. Under its influence, chastity appears as a school of the gift of the person. Self-mastery is ordered to the gift of self. Chastity leads him who practices it to become a witness to his neighbor of God's fidelity and loving kindness (CCC: 2346).

Our sexuality allows us to give ourselves to another in the most intimate and personal way. The gift of ourselves to our spouses demands self-mastery:

in marriage we promise to be faithful for life. This means not allowing ourselves to be tempted away from our spouse by any other person.

THE SAME SELF-MASTERY is involved in the vocations of priestly and religious life. These callings involve celibacy, offering God the exclusive gift of their sexuality. Does this mean they give up their sexuality? No! The self-mastery they practice is similar to that of married couples: it is a *gift of self*, in this case, directly to God.*

* CCC: 2349 quotes St. Ambrose on the equal dignity of various states of life: "There are three forms of the virtue of chastity: the first is that of spouses, the second that of widows, and the third that of virgins. We do not praise any one of them to the exclusion of the others.... This is what makes for the richness of the discipline of the Church."

Their sexuality still exists; their sexual feelings nurture their vocations as well. The priest or Religious can "witness to his neighbor of God's fidelity and loving kindness" because the virtue of chastity is also "a gift from God, a *grace*, a fruit of spiritual effort" (CCC: 2345).

Chastity does not suppress our sexuality, it *integrates* our sexuality. It brings the sexual powers of love and life into harmony with God. Misuse of sexuality harms your personality, but the proper use of our sexual powers, according to our vocation in life, *completes* our personality. We were made sexual beings for a purpose: to increase and multiply—not only the human race, but our own happiness in serving God and each other.

People may try to tell you that your Church's teachings on sexual morality are old-fashioned and no longer apply. They may try to convince you that these teachings reflect a hatred of our sexual nature, or that the chastity they uphold is impossible to live. In their own ignorance, they may even say that the Church is out-of-touch with modern science and unable to understand your sexuality.

I hope that what I have shared with you will help you appreciate that the Church wants you to experience great sexual happiness. The only way to real happiness is to live according to God's plan. After all, He made us, knows what's best for us, and loves us beyond imagining.

Contraception and Abortion

CONTRACEPTION is a catch-all phrase for a number of unnatural and immoral forms of birth control. The barrier methods (condom, diaphragms, sponges, etc.) are true contraceptives that seek to prevent conception from occuring by preventing the sperm from reaching the egg.

Generally speaking, in *contraceptive acts*, people tamper with the act of intercourse in order to enjoy sex while preventing the generation of new life.

Abortion kills the life already conceived and seeking to implant (or already implanted) in the mother's womb. Part of the evil of contraception is that it tempts couples to the greater evil of abortion. Once couples reject the possibility of new life in the act of intercourse, they become more willing to risk abortion.

Hormonal birth control drugs or chemicals typically act in any one of three ways. Sometimes they act as a contraceptive, preventing sperm from reaching the egg. Sometimes they prevent ovulation, the release of the egg. Sometimes they abort a newly conceived baby by preventing it from implanting in the womb.

The Pill, Norplant, and Depro-Provera are all forms of hormonal birth control, and they all have the potential to cause an early abortion in any given women in any given cycle.

Sterilization is surgery in which healthy sexual organs are mutilated for birth control purposes. In a vasectomy, a man's sperm passageways are cut so that sperm cannot be ejaculated. In a tubal ligation, the woman's Fallopian tubes are blocked or cut so that the egg cannot reach the place where conception occurs.

Sterilization is wrong not only because it is contraceptive, but because the operation mutilates the body, which is a sin against the Fifth Commandment. The removal of a diseased bodily organ is a different matter. This is permitted, but only for the higher purpose of saving life itself.

We are given our bodies by God, who has ultimate dominion over them. Those who say, "It's my body, I'll do what I want with it" deny this higher authority.*

A desire to limit the number of children, however legitimate, does not justify the use of an immoral means (CCC: 2399).

"Contraception, insistently propagated today, contrasts with these Christian ideals and these moral norms of which the Church is teacher. This fact renders still more urgent the necessity of transmitting to the young at an appropriate age the teaching of the Church on artificial means of contraception, and the reasons for such teaching, so that the young may be prepared for responsible marriage, full of love and open to life" ("Educational Guidance in Human Love," §62).

"According to Christian tradition...and as right reason also recognizes, the moral order of sexuality involves such high values of human life that every direct violation of this order is objectively serious" (*Persona Humana,* §10).

Note that the *serious* nature of violating the moral order of sexuality is due the high dignity of the gift that is being sinned against. This does not rule out the possibility that the sinner's guilt may be lessened due to an "imperfection" of the will. Mortal sin involves "serious matter," full knowledge of the act being contemplated, and full consent of the will. If the will does not perfectly, or fully consent to an act, it is called an "imperfect" will. See p. 229 for more on this subject.

* "Do you not know that your body is a temple of the Holy Spirit within you, which you have from God? You are not your own; you were bought with a price. So glorify God in your body" (1 Cor. 6:19-20).

Human Sexuality for Boys

Note to Parents

DISCUSSING THE PHYSICAL CHANGES OF PUBERTY often intimidates parents. It can be embarrassing to discuss intimate subjects both because we fear giving a wrong impression about human sexuality and because we have a natural modesty about these matters. Such modesty is a good thing; it is a fruit of the Holy Spirit.[1]

A dignified presentation of this material need not be immodest.

This instruction is a parent's duty, not a task to be turned over to others.* God is lavish with the graces of the Sacrament of Matrimony. He will provide you, as a parent, all that you need to insure that you will do a good job. Draw on those graces with a short prayer before instructing your child in these matters.

*__Bold-faced type__ is used in passages referring to parental example and responsibility to respect the child's right not to have too much information too soon.

Too often our uneasiness about the physical aspects of sexuality obscures our primary concern for the spiritual aspect here. Your child is biologically preparing for parenthood. That will happen naturally all by itself. **What your child needs most is your witness to the dignity of the vocation of marriage.** The example you have given throughout your child's life has been the most important factor in his view of the vocation of spouse and parent.

It is normal to assume that most children will be called to the vocation of marriage, but we must not ignore the possibility of other vocations, such as priesthood, vowed religious life, or dedicated, chaste singlehood. Whether a boy wants to be a husband or a priest, it is important that you give a positive testimony to being a follower of Christ in your role as spouse and parent. This will help children discern more intelligently whatever calling God has for them.

We believe that parents are the best evaluators of when their children are ready for the information that follows. There is much controversy, especially among Catholic educators, whether a "latency period"† actually exists. There is encouragement from many so-called "experts" to err on the side of earlier education on sexual matters. "Better five years too early than two minutes too late," some people advise. However, there is no need for early biological information if there is early education in discipleship and Christian chastity.

† The "latency period" is a technical term that comes from the Freudian school of psychology. We use the term here in a more colloquial sense in which it refers to the years before puberty when children have no interest in sexual matters in general and especially have no romantic interest in members of the opposite sex. Another term commonly used for this period is the "years of innocence."

[1]The Fruits of the Holy Spirit are good acts whose nature is to give joy to the virtuous. The Fruits of the Holy Spirit are "love, joy, peace, patience, kindness, goodness, faithfulness, gentleness, self-control" (CCC:736, see Galatians 5:22 and 23). The classic listing of these was slightly different: Charity, Joy, Peace, Patience, Long-sufferingness, Goodness, Kindness, Gentleness, Faithfulness, Modesty, Continency, and Chastity. See pp. 313-314 of the curriculum for more.

We believe that such a decision is the parents' decision in any case. Catholic educators can serve parents best by advising the need for a talk on detailed sexual matters when they suspect this need from classroom observation. They can also provide materials, such as this booklet, that will help organize the facts in a manner that also shows the richness and beauty of Catholic teaching concerning sexual morality.

When it comes to matters of faith, parents are the primary and most influential teachers of their children. A parent who does not consider it an obligation to attend Mass will raise children who fail to take seriously the commandment to honor the Sabbath. A parent's example concerning the Sixth and Ninth Commandments* is no less convincing. Pastors and educators perform an invaluable service in helping parents fulfill their "mission" to educate their children.

As the Second Vatican Council noted, in this mission parents "should realize that they are thereby cooperating with the love of God the Creator and are, in a certain sense, its interpreters" (*Gaudium et Spes*, 50).

We hope that this curriculum, especially this booklet, will help you interpret human sexuality in its full dignity and beauty, the gift of a loving God.

Nothing we can write in a booklet will *make* your child chaste.

Your honest example, proper teaching, and the power of the sacraments are most crucial in helping children remain chaste.

Chastity is a natural virtue. It is part of the cardinal virtue of Temperance. The holiness of Chastity was recognized by cultures long before the time of Christ. Chastity is also one of the Fruits of the Holy Spirit. This means that there are two ways of looking at Chastity. It is "natural." That is to say, we should not fear that expecting Chastity of a person is excessive. And Chastity can be more than merely avoiding impurity.†

At the same time, as a Fruit of the Holy Spirit, Chastity is the beautiful flowering of an inner grace. As the *Catechism of the Catholic Church* says, "Chastity means the successful integration of sexuality within the person and thus the inner unity of man in his bodily and spiritual being" (CCC: 2337). It is "a gift from God, a *grace*, a fruit of spiritual effort" (CCC: 2345).

Let us not underestimate the "effort" involved. The *Catechism* also notes that "Self-mastery is a *long and exacting work*. One can never consider it acquired once and for all" (cf. CCC: 2342).

This effort is not solely an individual responsibility.

> It also involves a *cultural effort*, for there is "an interdependence between personal betterment and the improvement of society." Chastity presupposes respect for the rights of the person, in particular the right to receive information and an education that respect the moral and spiritual dimensions of human life (CCC: 2344).

* See Catechism Articles 6 and 9 of Part 3 (2331-2400; 2514-2533).

In the Catholic counting of the Ten Commandments, the sixth and ninth commandments refer to sins against the marriage bond, specifically adultery, fornication, lust, and unnatural forms of birth control.

† "Nevertheless, the Lord's Redemption has made the positive practice of chastity into something that is really possible and a motive for joy, both for those who have the vocation to marriage (before, in the time of preparation, and afterwards, in the course of married life) as well as for those who have the gift of a special calling to the consecrated life.... So chastity is not be be understood as a repressive attitude" (*The Truth and Meaning of Human Sexuality*, §§3, 4).

IT IS OUR HOPE that nothing we have included in *The New Corinthians Curriculum*, and especially in this booklet, fails to respect the moral and spiritual dimensions of human life. If you deem anything presented here to be inappropriate, your decision is final in the matter. We hope that we are able to provide a resource for educating your child in Chastity.

Without the aid of the Holy Spirit, as St. Paul testifies, it is impossible to be chaste. When it comes to chastity, his observations are very sensible advice for parents as well as adolescents:

> Therefore let any one who thinks that he stands take heed lest he fall. No temptation has overtaken you that is not common to man. God is faithful, and he will not let you be tempted beyond your strength, but with the temptation will also provide the way of escape, that you may be able to endure it (1 Corinthians 10:12-13).

How Do You Tell When to Give This Information?

It is difficult to predict when a boy will enter puberty. For general purposes, the earliest age is usually given as 10, but some might not enter it until 14 for even 15. Some boys will experience a nocturnal emission before any other signs of puberty, such as body hair, facial blemishes, etc.

This is naturally a bit upsetting, and your reaction to the event means everything. It can be the "teachable moment" when you explain the basics of reproduction and the gift of fertility. Just explain that God created men this way and the body sloughs off excess sperm and semen and there is nothing wrong with him.

It is not wise to "celebrate" this experience. It is a significant stage of his development and brings with it a whole new range of responsibilities. It is not, however, the arrival of "manhood" in its most profound sense.

To overemphasize nocturnal emission in a positive sense might encourage a boy to masturbate. You may want to use this occasion to note the difference between nocturnal emission and masturbation, again, depending on his sensitivity to the subject.

It would be best to establish a continual dialogue with the child from an early age, answering questions as simply as possible when they arise. For a boy of six who asks where babies come from, it is enough to explain, "The baby lives in a special place beneath mom's tummy." At such an age the child's curiosity is easily satisfied.

For a boy approaching puberty the situation is different. It would be ideal if he were prepared to understand what is happening before his first nocturnal emission, but its impossible to predict Nature's timetable. If he knows that you will answer his questions honestly and openly, then you needn't worry much about whether you are giving information too early or too late.

There are ways to tell the onset of puberty.

Watch for any sudden change of personality. Many boys will become sullen, easily bored, or irritable as new hormones enter the system. Some parents note that boys become surly under the influence of testosterone.

Some boys become critical of everything, despairing, or untypically assertive in behavior.

Take this opportunity to start a long-running conversation on the topic of puberty. It is certainly not necessary to plow through all the subjects in this booklet. It is often best handled in a continuing dialogue over the course of your son's adolescence.

Topics for Boys

The following information is not meant to be read to nor by *your son. It is merely a suggested way for you to convey the information, a way of opening a dialogue with your child. Perhaps you have already communicated some of these points. Many sections concern subjects you may decide your child is not ready to hear about or will not need until later in your mutual dialogue. This dialogue should not be confined to one "talk" but should extend throughout the child's adolescence and into adulthood.*

"There's Something I'd Like to Tell You..."

SOON YOU WILL BE GOING THROUGH CHANGES as your body prepares to be an adult. I'd like to be the one to introduce you to this part of your life. I want you to know that I'll be here for you as you go through these changes and I want you to feel comfortable talking with me about these things.

Whether or not I'm too late doesn't matter. I want you to know that I'll be here for you as you go through these changes and I want you to feel comfortable talking with me about these things.

If you haven't started yet, soon your body will go through the many changes of puberty. They are all the result of the hormone *testosterone* now being released into your bloodstream. This hormone is manufactured when your *hypothalamus* produces a releasing hormone, telling the pituitary gland (the "master gland" of the body) that you have reached the right age.

Some boys enter puberty around age ten, most will reach it by age 16.

Don't be too concerned if you are lagging behind when it comes to these changes. We could all tell you stories about fellows who seemed to take forever to reach puberty.

Puberty starts when a chemical signal is sent to the *testicles*, located in the *scrotum*, to start producing *sperm cells.*

It is a complicated process, but it essentially means that you are beginning to make cells that contain half of what is needed to make a human being. Each sperm cell contains 23 *chromosomes.*

The mother's egg, which I'll describe in a few minutes, contains the other 23 chromosomes.

Chromosomes hold the genes that determine all our characteristics: our height, hair color, eye color, bone thickness, eyesight, and a million other things that make you a unique creation of God.

There will never be another person exactly like you.

ON THE PRACTICAL SIDE, the production of sperm will cause your scrotum to enlarge. This swelling can be uncomfortable at times and takes some getting used to. You will want to start wearing an athletic supporter when playing sports or performing strenuous work, especially heavy lifting.

Testosterone causes other sexual characteristics. Some of these include:

1. Your voice box (larynx) will enlarge, causing your voice to deepen. Sometimes during this process, your voice will fluctuate, break or squeak, which can be embarrassing.

2. Your muscles will develop more bulk and you will find yourself eating more to supply the calories necessary for this. Try to eat a well-balanced diet so you don't accumulate too many fat cells.

3. You may go through dramatic growth spurts, adding inches to your height seemingly overnight. You will outgrow clothes sooner, and you may be a little clumsy for a while. Your arms and legs aren't the same size they were a short time ago and it is difficult to get used to them. You may feel "growing pains" as the tendons and ligaments in your joints stretch.

4. The changes in your body's chemistry can also produce a change in the makeup of the oils (sebum) that lubricate your skin. For a while it becomes more difficult for those oils to reach the surface layer and exit the openings, or pores, of the skin. This blockage makes a good environment for the bacteria that are normally found on the surface of the skin. A pimple forms.

This condition is called acne and it is a normal part of going through puberty. If you handle or squeeze the pimples, you risk spreading the bacteria in high concentrations to other pores. Infection can worsen along with discoloration. Scabs form to protect and aid in healing the damaged skin. If these are picked as well, scar tissue may form.

The best treatment for acne is to wash your face once or twice a day with a skin cleanser. Be sure to drink enough water, which helps keep skin healthy.

Acne usually goes away by the late teens or early twenties.

5. Testosterone also causes the release of *pheromones* in sweat, which can cause body odor. Bathe or shower after heavy exercise, and use a deodorant. During hot weather bathe or shower at least daily.

6. You will notice pubic hair appearing around the genitals, under your arms, on the chest, back and legs, and eventually on your face. Don't feel less manly because some guy you know has a full beard at 16. God knows when you need to develop this trait.

The Other Half

You may wish to use the diagram on p. 10 while discussing the following material.

AT THE AGE OF PUBERTY young women undergo their own sexual development. Their fertility is very different from yours. It moves in a cycle that is directed by the hormone called *estrogen*. This cycle usually takes somewhere between 26 and 40 days. Here's how it works:

1. When a girl reaches a certain physical maturity, two small organs called *ovaries*, located in the lower abdomen, begin to prepare eggs (*ovum*). An ovary is about the size of an almond. One (or possibly two) of these eggs ripens and is released in the course of a few weeks. The egg passes from the ovary into the Fallopian tube, which connects with the womb, or *uterus*.
2. While the egg is ripening, it causes the hormone estrogen to be released.
3. During the cycle the lining of the uterus prepares for pregnancy. A rich supply of blood is needed for a baby to attach to the wall of the womb and live. If no pregnancy occurs, this lining is shed at the end of the cycle in what is called *menses* or *menstruation*.
4. The menses, or bleeding, is also known as a *period*, since it occurs periodically—normally every 26-34 days. Women enter puberty when they experience their first period.

During puberty, girls also undergo physical changes. In addition to some changes similar to yours, the hips of the young woman begin to broaden to make room for carrying a baby. Breast tissue develops, including glands that will produce milk once a baby is born.

THE PHYSICAL CHANGES that indicate that a girl has become capable of bearing children attract male interest. Your sexual interest is stimulated primarily by sight. Female sexual attraction is not stimulated in this way, and often young women are not aware of this. They may dress or act immodestly, especially if they haven't been told about this difference between them and boys.

It is important, as a young Catholic male, to recognize that whether a girl is being intentionally immodest or not, it is your *responsibility never to provoke or encourage or entertain erotic thoughts*.

This includes your responsibility to dress and act modestly yourself. Also, you must never intentionally look at pornographic magazines, films, or videos, or listen to sexually enticing songs, lyrics, or jokes. Novels that describe sexual scenes are never to be read. All of these things are "occasions of sin."* That is, they provide a temptation to violate the Sixth and Ninth Commandments against lustful thought and behavior.

* For more on the "Occasions of Sin" see page 45.

The Proper Use of Sexuality†

† First read the section, "The Marital Embrace," pp. 8-9.

IN ANIMALS, the actions that cause the conception of a baby are driven by instinct. In humans, there is more to it than instincts and hormones. We are created in God's image, which means that we have wills. We can control our actions, even act contrary to Nature. We act contrary to Nature by sinning, misusing God's gift of sexuality.

All of us are called to chastity, whether we are priests or parents, single people or widowers. Chastity is the virtue by which a person is able to place sexuality in the service of authentic love as God has intended. It is described in the Catechism, section 2338: "The chaste person maintains the integrity of the powers of life and love placed in him" (by God).

We are made sexual beings—males—and this is essential to who we are. This is not to say that your sexual organs are the most important aspect of your being. The *Machismo* (Macho) attitude of some cultures overemphasizes masculinity this way, to the point of disrespecting the equal dignity of women.

Chastity gives a man the skill of "self-mastery," being in control of how he functions as a sexual being. The "Macho Man" is controlled by his sexual needs, a fact he may try to disguise by bullying or controlling those weaker than himself physically.

On the other hand, it is not good to be ashamed of your sexuality. God creates the male body with fatherhood in mind. Fatherhood means being allowed to cooperate with God in the procreation of a child. It also means accepting the responsibility to provide for a family and train children in the faith. This is a deep, lifelong commitment, which a man takes on as a calling from God.

A man may also be called to priesthood, religious life, or dedicated single celibacy. In offering back to God the gift of sexual intercourse, a celibate man does not give up being a male.

Sexuality is just as important to being a priest or single man as it is in a marriage. The sexual drive that enriches a husband's love for his wife can be turned into a source of energy and desire to serve others out of love for God. Success in any vocation requires chastity, just as it requires all the other virtues of the Christian life.

Even those who feel called to celibacy will have sexual urges. For young men it is not unusual to experience an *erection* (the stiffening of the penis). This may happen for no apparent reason. This can be confusing, but it has a natural physical explanation.

What is an Erection?

There is a one-way valve located in the penis that shuts off when signalled by the brain. Blood entering the spongy tissue of the penis is retained causing the erection. This will usually go away by itself in a couple of minutes.

If the erection is due to having seen or heard something "sexy," you should start taking responsibility not to expose yourself to these things in the future. This is called "having custody of your eyes and ears." Temptations can assault a boy without warning. These are not his fault, but when a boy *invites* things to tempt him—music or videos or magazines—it is seriously sinful. He is telling God, "I'll just check this out. You get lost for a while."

Sometimes an erection will occur—truly—for no reason. Upon waking a boy will sometimes experience an erection due to the pressure of a full bladder. The remedy for this is to go to the bathroom immediately. Do not dwell on this sign of your sexuality, especially do not fondle or rub the penis to produce sexual pleasure.

This is called *masturbation* and it is seriously sinful. The release of semen in what is called an *orgasm* is meant to take place only in marital intercourse.

Nocturnal Emission and Masturbation

Your body makes about 500 microscopic sperm cells each minute. They are so small you needn't worry about the great numbers involved, you won't explode! God has designed a way of dealing with the surplus.

Over the course of time the scrotum will release surplus sperm and semen (the fluid that carries the sperm). It is the body's way of dealing with an excess. This flushing of the system usually occurs at night.

This is called a *nocturnal emission* (nocturne, night). This is not the same as masturbation and is *not physically or morally harmful.* We are not responsible for unconscious acts.

Masturbation, however, involves deliberately entertaining erotic thoughts and willfully stimulating an erection, even to the point of releasing sperm in an orgasm.

Sometimes there will be erotic (sexy) dreams during a nocturnal emission. This is not the same as "lusting," which involves a deliberate contemplation of sexual activity with another person. A nocturnal emission is natural to our state as males and will probably occur every month or so. It is not a dirty thing, but rather a sign that the sexual organs are in working order.

The reality of nocturnal emission explains why there is nothing to the argument that "men have to have sex" because of an oversurplus of sperm. There is no physical excuse for masturbation or other voluntary acts that result in orgasm outside of the marital embrace.

It is within marriage that God intends sexual arousal and procreation to occur. To intentionally separate the act of sexual orgasm from any possibility of conceiving a child is to separate what God joined when He fashioned our sexuality.

God intended marriage, love, and life to be joined in the marriage act. Outside marriage, sexual intercourse is *untruthful, unwise, and unjust* (especially to any children involved).

A man without self-control is like a city broken into and left without walls.

—Proverbs 25: 28

* See Glossary p. 320.

BECAUSE I LOVE YOU, I must warn you against masturbation, a temptation that often arrives during times of great stress—and adolescence can be one of the most stressful times in your life. The danger of masturbation is not physical; it is a spiritual danger. This is an objectively evil act.* That means it is wrong to do it no matter what moves you to do it. It is a bad habit to start and a worse one to break.

Sexual feelings can be used just like a drug. They can be generated by the act of masturbation as well as by intercourse. But this is wrong.

Any stimulation of the sexual organs outside marriage is immoral, and masturbation totally separates love from life.

The Church has always taught that seeking sexual pleasure for itself is lust, a capital sin (CCC: 2351). We are never to use our bodies or another person's merely to satisfy lust. The wonderful feelings of our sexuality are intended to help us love our wives more deeply.

Masturbation, just as with sex outside marriage, cannot do this. It is a serious sin (CCC: 2352). A habit of masturbating can form that is difficult to break. That may have a bad effect on a future marriage, since it establishes a precedent of engaging in sexual pleasure apart from the marital embrace.

At times when you are angry, feel bad about yourself, lonely, or bored, the temptation may arise to masturbate. It never helps anything, but only makes you feel worse. The struggle in life is to love others, and masturbation takes away the drive that would send our love outside ourselves to others.

If you are ever tempted to masturbate, resist it with all your might. *Stop immediately* whatever you are doing that has aroused you. Do something different. Often strenuous exercise can "work off" the temptation.

This is not merely a physical problem. Pray for help, but remember to immediately change the situation so that you don't entertain the temptation. Often temptation occurs after waking in the middle of the night with an erection due to a full bladder. As I said before, the solution to the problem, most often is go to the bathroom.

St. Paul's advice is my advice, "Shun immorality. Every other sin which a man commits is outside the body; but the immoral man sins against his own body. Do you not know that your body is a temple of the Holy Spirit within you, which you have from God? You are not your own; you were bought with a price. So glorify God in your body" (1 Corinthians 6: 18-20).

See note on page 22 about discussing this topic with your son.

Homosexuality

Two people of the same sex cannot have true sexual intercourse. Some men are attracted to men, some women to women. There are numerous theories about why this happens, but the sexual acts they perform are contrary to nature and offensive to God.* Many in our society see no difference between these homosexual acts and married, or heterosexual, love. They believe that if two homosexuals feel love for each other, the nature of their sexual copulation doesn't matter.

We believe the Church has received her teaching on sexual love directly from God, Who is Love. The Church cannot be wrong, but she is often misunderstood. Homosexual copulation is contrary to nature. In the Scriptures, the sin of sodomy is condemned as one of the "sins that cry to heaven."†

Sodomy is generally defined as any unnatural sexual relations. More specifically, it is any sexual relations between two males.‡

With homosexuals, however, there is no possibility of their relations resulting in life. They are by nature closed to life.

Nevertheless, because God calls everyone to conversion and repentance, the Church urges that homosexuals be "accepted with respect, compassion, and sensitivity. Every sign of unjust discrimination in their regard should be avoided" (CCC: 2358).

As Christians, we believe that the saddest thing to contemplate is being separated from Jesus by sin. There is no "gay" life-style apart from Jesus. God calls everyone to eternal happiness, but only the "pure in heart" will see God (Matthew 5:8).

Homosexuals, too, are called to embrace the chastity expected of all followers of Christ. This is difficult, and we are not to make it even more difficult for them by our hatred. This will only have the effect of turning them away from the Truth, Jesus, Who alone sets us free from sin.

We hate the sin, never the sinner.

* "Basing itself on Sacred Scripture, which presents homosexual acts as acts of grave depravity, tradition has always declared that 'homosexual acts are intrinsically disordered.' They are contrary to the natural law. They close the sexual act to the gift of life. They do not proceed from a genuine affective and sexual complementarity. Under no circumstances can they be approved" (CCC: 2357).

† See CCC: 1867.
The other sins that cry to heaven for punishment are willful murder, oppression of the poor, widows and orphans, and defrauding laborers.

‡Rejection of the sin of sodomy is not just a "Catholic" matter. Contraception was unanimously condemned by all Christian denominations as a form of marital sodomy, the sin of Onan (see Genesis 38:8-10). This unanimity held until 1930 when the Anglican Bishops at the Council of Lambeth approved use of some forms of contraception for married couples in difficult situations. For more information on the traditional Protestant view, read *The Bible and Birth Control* by Charles Provan, available from The Couple to Couple League, 1-800-745-8252.2.

Homosexual persons are called to chastity. By the virtues of self-mastery that teach them inner freedom, at times by the support of disinterested friendship, by prayer and sacramental grace, they can and should gradually and resolutely approach Christian perfection.

— CCC: 2359

Emotional Changes

TESTOSTERONE IS A MALE HORMONE; women have very little of it. It is the hormone men need to make them strong and vigorous. It not only makes the male body larger and more powerful, it also has psychological effects on you.

When you are getting your first increases of this hormone, it can take you by surprise. You might experience strange aches and pains, feel down one minute and up the next. Your temper might flare up unexpectedly because of it. Things can seem to get out of control.

As you approached the age of puberty, you learned to express your emotions in more mature way. Now it will seem as though you wasted your time. Anybody and anything can just "seem stupid" all of a sudden, and you have a hard time figuring out why.

Realize that this might be due to the effect of a new hormone. This is a time when you are being called to learn how to understand your emotions and the way they connect with your reason and will.* You will learn about your temper—as well as your sexuality. You will find out about your *character*.

* "In themselves passions are neither good nor evil. They are morally qualified only to the extent that they effectively engage reason and will.... Passions are morally good when they contribute to a good action, evil in the opposite case" (CCC: 1767-1768).

A man's character is different from his personality or his talents. His personality is partly inherited, partly the result of his life experiences. His talents come from having the right genes, the right training, and the right opportunities. A man's character, however, is the combination of everything he is and what he chooses to do with them. He can be a genius at math or bankrobbing. His character determines which.

A person is a combination of a body, which dies, and a soul, which doesn't (CCC: 362). The soul "animates" the body and together they share in the "dignity of the image of God" (CCC: 364). The soul contains the abilities to think and feel, to judge and then act. Character is the result of your judgment about what is good or evil, and your actions.

When you were a baby, feelings and instincts directed your actions. A baby needs a diaper change, but he doesn't know that. He feels wet, his bottom is irritated. He cries. But he doesn't understand that parents have ear drums that receive sound vibrations. His cry is a reflex.

As you got older, you learned more about things and why they upset you. Your emotions called problems to your attention and your mind solved them.

If your emotions got out of hand, you found it hard to make a sound judgment. You figured out what those emotions were telling you.

At age four you cried because you were overtired and it told us you needed to get to bed. Now you yawn, or feel a little crabby, and you look at the clock. It's late, so you start getting ready for bed. If you want to stay up later, you might try especially hard to hide your feelings so we won't tell you to go to bed. At the same time, you realize you'll need extra sleep. There are many judgments being weighed in all this.

When the hormones of adolescence cause you to be crabby "for no reason," it tears apart all the work you have been doing. This might get you down even further. Understand that I appreciate the struggle you are going through. Let me know how you're feeling, we can talk these things out.

Alcohol and Drugs

Teens have to endure a lot of frustration. It is frustrating to have to wait so long for independence. You want to find out who you are, but you're not quite sure you'll like what you discover. You don't want to be just another face in the crowd, but peer pressure keeps you from daring to be different. You want to be cool, but sometimes it feels like you've lost track of who you really are. Who wouldn't be confused and frustrated?

Your emotions are there for a reason. Anger is meant to energize your will to attack whatever threatens you. Fear motivates you to flee. Since physically fighting or fleeing our problems isn't often acceptable, we end up having to swallow our emotions. We end up depressed, like animals in cages unable to exert our wills.

Many young men fall into a trap. They begin to abuse their bodies with tobacco, alcohol, marijuana, and other drugs. It might start out as a way for them to show their independence, but it becomes a form of slavery.

Alcohol and many other drugs can be used as anesthetics—to kill pain. It isn't hard to see how tempting this could be to someone who is going through the emotions of adolescence.

Emotions can be frightening and painful. Drugs can mask them, turn them around, or even turn them off. They can provide a temporary feeling of well-being, a fantasy not based in reality.

The tragedy of drugs is that they give a false sense of hope. When things bother us, we should take our concerns to Jesus in prayer. He is our hope and His Truth sets us free. When we look for a quick solution in drugs, we buy into a lie.

Drugs can produce psychological addiction. Some people even become *psychologically* addicted to eating as a way of relieving stress and getting a temporary good feeling. The so-called "legal drugs," alcohol and nicotine, also cause a *physical* addiction in a relatively short time. Illegal drugs are usually much more addictive and have profound effects on a person's moods. "Crack" cocaine is so addictive that even a single use may be addictive.

The addict finds that he is unable to stop abusing his body because his happiness rests so completely on the lie he has accepted.

There are proper uses for many substances, but none for addictive and illegal drugs. They are a snare set to entrap you and ruin your life.

The rule for food and drink is to use them in moderation. This is the virtue of temperance.

The Catechism states:

> The virtue of temperance disposes us *to avoid every kind of excess*: the abuse of food, alcohol, tobacco, or medicine. Those incur grave guilt who, by drunkenness or a love of speed, endanger their own and others' safety on the road, at sea, or in the air.
>
> The *use of drugs* inflicts very grave damage on human health and life. Their use, except on strictly therapeutic grounds, is a grave offense. Clandestine [secretive] production of and trafficking in drugs are scandalous practices. They constitute direct cooperation in evil, since they encourage people to practices gravely contrary to the moral law (CCC: 2290-2291).

Many people in our culture make light of drug use. They glamorize the "fast life" of wild parties, reckless driving, and irresponsible actions. They do not tell you about the pain and cost of trading the hope of heaven for the lie of "getting high." It is a depressing thing, and the reason they use drugs in the first place is to avoid depression. Don't be fooled. There can be no lasting joy when it involves offending God. Place your trust in Him: "For the Lord will be your confidence and will keep your foot from being caught" (Proverbs 3:26).

A Final Word

YOUR FEELINGS ARE INTENDED FOR A GOOD PURPOSE, including your sexual feelings. They are part of the way God made you as a human being. They incline you to take on the role of a loving spouse and father. When these feelings occur within the context of marriage, great good arises, not only for the couple and their children, but for society as well. A chaste marriage reflects the great love God has for us. He wants our sexuality to be for us a preview of the complete joy of heaven.

Being chaste does not mean denying our sexuality. It means understanding and desiring God's plan for our sexuality, which is to generate love. With that understanding and desire come self-mastery.

The Catechism explains it well:

> Charity is the *form* of all the virtues. Under its influence, chastity appears as a school of the gift of the person. Self-mastery is ordered to the gift of self. Chastity leads him who practices it to become a witness to his neighbor of God's fidelity and loving kindness (CCC: 2346).

OUR SEXUALITY ALLOWS US TO GIVE OURSELVES to another in the most intimate and personal way. The gift of ourselves to our spouses demands self-mastery, because with marriage we promise to be faithful for life. This means not allowing ourselves to be tempted away from our spouse by any other person.

The same sort of self-mastery is involved in the vocations of priestly and religious life. These callings involve celibacy, offering God the exclusive gift of their sexuality. Does this mean they give up their sexuality? No! The self-mastery they practice is like that of married couples: it is a *gift of self*, in this case, a total gift given directly to God.* Their sexuality still exists; their sexual feelings nurture their vocations as well.

The priest or Religious can "witness to his neighbor of God's fidelity and loving kindness" because the virtue of chastity is also "a gift from God, a *grace*, a fruit of spiritual effort" (CCC: 2345).

Chastity does not suppress our sexuality, it *integrates* our sexuality. It brings the sexual powers of love and life into harmony with God. Misuse of sexuality harms your personality, but the proper use of our sexual powers, according to our vocation in life, *completes* our personality. We have been made sexual beings for a purpose: to increase and multiply—not only the human race, but our own happiness in serving God and each other.

People may try to tell you that your Church's teachings on sexual morality are old-fashioned and no longer apply. They may try to convince you that these teachings reflect a hatred of our sexual nature, or that the chastity they uphold is impossible to live. In their ignorance, they may even say that the Church is out-of-touch with modern science and unable to understand your sexuality.

I hope that what I have shared with you will help you appreciate that the Church wants you to experience great happiness. That happiness will be proportionate to your self-mastery and, if you marry, to the degree of mutual self-giving in your marriage.

In brief, that happiness is to cooperate with God in His plan for love and life.

* CCC: 2349 quotes St. Ambrose on the equal dignity of various states of life:

"There are three forms of the virtue of chastity: the first is that of spouses, the second that of widows, and the third that of virgins.

"We do not praise any one of them to the exclusion of the others....

"This is what makes for the richness of the discipline of the Church."

Contraception and Abortion

"Contraception, insistently propagated today, contrasts with these Christian ideals and these moral norms of which the Church is teacher. This fact renders still more urgent the necessity of transmitting to the young at an appropriate age the teaching of the Church on artificial means of contraception, and the reasons for such teaching, so that the young may be prepared for responsible marriage, full of love and open to life" ("Educational Guidance in Human Love," §62).

CONTRACEPTION AND STERILIZATION are immoral forms of birth control. Contraceptives try to prevent the sperm from reaching the egg. *Sterilization* is surgery in which healthy bodily organs are mutilated for birth control purposes. In a vasectomy, the man's body is mutilated so that sperm cannot be ejaculated. In a tubal ligation, the woman's Fallopian tubes are blocked or cut so that the egg cannot reach the place where conception occurs.

In *contraception*, people tamper with the act of intercourse in order to enjoy sex while preventing the generation of new life. *Abortion* kills the life already conceived and seeking to implant (or already implanted) in the mother's womb.

Some methods of contraception may cause early abortions when they fail to prevent conception by preventing a newly conceived baby from implanting in the womb. These are called *abortifacients*.

"According to Christian tradition...and as right reason also recognizes, the moral order of sexuality involves such high values of human life that every direct violation of this order is objectively serious" (*Persona Humana,* §10).

Note that the *serious* nature of violating the moral order of sexuality is due the high dignity of the gift that is being sinned against. This does not rule out the possibility that the sinner's guilt may be lessened due to an "imperfection" of the will. Mortal sin involves "serious matter," full knowledge of the act being contemplated, and full consent of the will. If the will does not perfectly, or fully consent to an act, it is called an "imperfect" will.

See p. 229 for more on this subject.

For example, every form of the birth control Pill and other forms of chemical or hormonal birth control can cause an early abortion in any woman in any menstrual cycle. One of the evils of contraception is that it prepares couples to contemplate the greater evil of abortion should a "surprise pregnancy" take place. Once couples have rejected the possibility of new life in the act of intercourse, they are all the more willing to risk abortion.

Sterilization is wrong not only because it is contraceptive. The sterilization operation mutilates the body, a sin against the Fifth Commandment. We are given our bodies by God, who has ultimate dominion over them.

Those who say, "It's my body, I'll do what I want with it" deny this higher authority.* The removal of a bodily organ is permitted only for the higher purpose of saving life itself.

A desire to limit the number of children, however legitimate, does not justify the use of an immoral means (CCC: 2399).

* "Do you not know that your body is a temple of the Holy Spirit within you, which you have from God? You are not your own; you were bought with a price. So glorify God in your body" (1 Cor. 6:19-20).

Faced with so many opposing points of view, and a widespread rejection of sound doctrine concerning human life, we can feel that Paul's entreaty to Timothy is also addressed to us: "Preach the word, be urgent in season and out of season, convince, rebuke, and exhort, be unfailing in patience and in teaching."

—John Paul II,* Evangelium Vitae, *§82

Note: This section is intended for both boys and girls

Occasions of Sin

The way of the wicked is like deep darkness; they do not know over what they stumble. Proverbs 4:19

SIN IS THE GREATEST EVIL in the world because it offends God, the Creator of the world.

Mortal sin "results in the loss of charity and the privation of sanctifying grace, that is, of the state of grace. If it is not redeemed by repentance and God's forgiveness, it causes exclusion from Christ's kingdom and the eternal death of hell, for our freedom has the power to make choices forever, with no turning back" (CCC: 1861). In other words, mortal sin leads to eternal damnation.

If you are serious about avoiding sin, then you must be serious about avoiding whatever you know tempts you to sin.* These are called "occasions of sin."

Definition: An occasion of sin is any outside influence that offers one an opportunity or enticement to sin.

An occasion of sin may be a person, a thing, or a place (situation, neighborhood, work place, etc.).

Occasions of sin may be remote or near.

— A remote occasion of sin is one in which you meet with a slight danger of sinning.

— A near occasion of sin is one in which a person almost always sins.

It is a principle of Catholic morality that it is a sin to *freely* place yourself in a near occasion of sin. To do so is the same as *willing* the particular sin that such occasions bring on. Jesus said, "You have heard that it was said, 'You shall not commit adultery.' But I say to you that every one who looks at a woman lustfully has already committed adultery with her in his heart" (Matthew 5:28).

Example: If a boy knows that being alone with his girlfriend will most likely lead to sexual activity, he must avoid being alone with her. If he arranges to do so, he has placed himself in a near occasion of sin. He has already sinned. Dating the girl in a group situation may be a remote occasion of sin, since they may be

* CCC: 2338 reads:

"The chaste person maintains the integrity of the powers of life and love placed in him. This integrity ensures the unity of the person; it is opposed to any behavior that would impair it. It tolerates neither a double life nor duplicity in speech."

The *Catechism* then refers to Jesus saying in Matthew 5:37:

"Let what you say be simply 'Yes' or 'No'; anything more than this comes from evil."

To say you hate the sin and accept an invitation to do it is to be a hypocrite.

tempted to slip away. Single dating for young people who are not ready to marry is frequently a near occasion of sin, and must be avoided.*

Example: If a girl knows that going with certain friends after school almost always means drinking alcohol, she has to avoid their company. Their company *at* school may be a remote occasion of sin. Their company *after* school is a near occasion of sin. She may not be able to avoid the first, but she must avoid the second.

If a near occasion of sin cannot be avoided, we are to make it remote through prayer, frequenting the sacraments, and self discipline.†

Example: A man finds that fellow employees in the workplace present a temptation to some sin (impure speech, drug use, disrespect for the employer, you name it). He may not be able to change the situation by transferring to another department, changing jobs, or another means. His only recourse is to change himself. Maybe he could attend Mass in the mornings before work. Maybe he could frequent the Sacrament of Penance every week until his co-workers no longer present a temptation to him. Maybe he could challenge himself to say a silent prayer whenever he becomes tempted to join in the sinful speech, or spend his coffee break taking a meditative walk instead of abusing his body with drugs or alcohol.

TELEVISION AND FILMS ARE COMMON OCCASIONS OF SIN for American teens. If certain TV programs have been causing temptations in your life, either plan to avoid them or avoid television. If you find that merely turning on the set leads you to watching bad programs, then turning on the set is a near occasion of sin.

Self-discipline, such as temporarily "fasting" from legitimate pleasures,‡ will strengthen your character. Self-mastery helps you withstand temptations and reduces the number of near occasions of sin in your life. This is part of the reason for the Lenten times of fast and abstinence. Without the distraction from our normal, legitimate pleasures, we can focus on the important thing in life: becoming more like Christ.

It may be that you will be capable someday of watching TV with only a very slight temptation to sin. Don't give up on the future. The "friend" you worry about losing may be impressed by the change in your life. He or she may ask you about your faith, he or she may become a true friend in the Lord instead of an occasion of sin in your life.

Sexually Transmitted Diseases (STDs)

THERE ARE OVER 50 DISEASES that are contracted primarily by sexual intercourse. They are called STDs. Some of these are minor inconveniences, causing sores, itching, and embarrassment. Others are serious, causing damage to the reproductive system, infertility, and even death to the sufferer.

* "The virtue of chastity blossoms in *friendship....* Chastity is expressed notably in *friendship with one's neighbor.* Whether it develops between persons of the same or opposite sex, friendship represents a great good for all" (CCC: 2347). The goal of "dating" should be the cultivation of friendship, chaste friendship.

† CCC: 2340 reads:
"Whoever wants to remain faithful to his baptismal promises and resist temptations will want to adopt the *means* of doing so: self-knowledge, practice of an ascesis adapted to the situations that confront him, obedience to God's commandments, exercise of the moral virtues, and fidelity to prayer."
The unfamiliar expression "practice of an ascesis adapted to the situations" is a more precise way of saying self-discipline.

‡ Avoiding those persons, places, or things that tempt you to evil is not "fasting," but merely obeying the commandments. Fasting, as a religious practice, means giving up something that is otherwise good or morally neutral.

According to some sources, nearly 50 million Americans have one or another STD.[1] This does not include those infected by AIDS, which is also sexually contagious and as yet incurable and fatal. Sexually transmitted diseases are contagious only through sexual intimacy. If two people marry who have never had sexual relations with anyone else, they are not at risk from STDs.

Some STDs are contracted by babies when they are born. For example, a disease such as herpes can be passed from an infected mother to her baby, causing blindness and brain damage. It is tragic that such a thing should happen to an innocent child. If the child escapes the worst effects of some diseases, he will grow up knowing that, should he marry, he will put his beloved spouse at risk. Still, if they both remained chaste within marriage, the disease would be contained. Their children could be delivered surgically so that the STD would not be passed down to yet another generation.

Chastity is the only cure for STDs. If everyone behaved chastely, respecting the gift of sexuality and reserving it to its proper place—within a faithful marriage—STDs would be as rare as smallpox, and soon extinct.

Whether or not these diseases are a "judgment" from God, intended as punishment on sinful uses of sexuality, they are certainly a reminder that God's law concerning chastity was revealed to us for our own good. The diseases of unchastity attack the body, but the greatest risk from immoral sexual acts goes much further than disfigurement, illness, or even death. Sin and the possibility of an eternal separation from God is by far the most tragic thing that can happen.

There are devices (like condoms) that may ward off the physical effects of unchastity for a while, but they are useless against the spiritual devastation of violating God's truth about the meaning of human sexuality. People can hope for cures and wonder drugs that will protect them from STDs, but this is like a compulsive gambler hoping that next week's lottery will make up for betraying his family this week by blowing the rent money. He may be able to pay his debts, but the damage to his relationship with his wife and children is not so easily remedied. As Jesus asked, "For what shall it profit a man, if he gain the whole world, and suffer the loss of his soul?"†

The physical suffering of STDs should give us reason to avoid the sins of unchastity. If we are only concerned with the physical pain, however, we may be tempted to merely weigh pleasure against pain and ignore the fact that God is calling us to happiness through chastity.

By remaining chaste we not only avoid physical disease and the mental torment of promiscuous relationships, we are left free to enjoy the happiness God intended for us as sexual beings. We are free to give the unblemished gift of ourselves in marriage or in consecrated life. There is no way to calculate the great graces available to the pure in heart, but Jesus has promised that those who remain pure "shall see God."

[1] *Facts in Brief: Teenage Sexual and Reproductive Behavior,* Alan Guttmacher Institute (New York) and the Centers for Disease Control (Atlanta), 1993.

It is not our intention to present here a "safe sex" course. Such an approach does little more than scandalize the innocent by directing the discussion of sexuality into the contemplation of the perverse. The Pontifical Council for the Family has urged that "...parents should offer well-reasoned arguments about the great value of chastity and show the intellectual and human weakness of theories that inspire permissive and hedonistic behavior. They will answer clearly, without giving excessive importance to pathological sexual problems" (TMHS, §96).

We believe the best "safe sex" argument lies in the positive encouragement to live chastely out of love for God.

An excellent reference on STDs is *Safe Sex: The doctor Examines the Realities of AIDS and Other STDs*, by Dr. Joseph S. McIlhaney, available through CCL, $8.95. Although his moral advice in some areas is inconsistent with Catholic teaching, his analysis of the myth of "safe sex" from the perspective of a Christian obstetrician-gynecologist is valuable and thorough.

† Mark 8:36, Douay-Rheims translation.

Glossary

Abortion is the deliberate killing of a human being before birth by any means, including chemical or hormonal drugs or devices. (CCC: 2270-2274)

Adultery refers to marital infidelity. When two partners, of whom at least one is married to another party, have sexual relations – even transient ones – they commit adultery. (CCC: 2380)

Chastity is the state in which a person successfully harmonizes sexuality with the purpose for which God intended it and also with God's calling for that person's life (or vocation). God's purpose for sexuality is to bring about children and to unite spouses more closely in marriage. His purpose for our lives is that we know, love, serve, and be happy with Him in Heaven. (CCC: 2337, 1721)

Contraception is the use of unnatural means to prevent the conception of a baby. All unnatural means of contraception are immoral. On the other hand, natural means of postponing conception (e.g., Natural Family Planning, breastfeeding) may be used by married persons "with the generosity appropriate to responsible parenthood." (CCC: 2366-2372)

Fornication is carnal union between an unmarried man and an unmarried woman (CCC: 2353).

Homosexuality refers to copulation between men or between women who experience an exclusive or predominant sexual attraction toward persons of the same sex. (CCC: 2357)

Lust is disordered desire for or inordinate enjoyment of sexual pleasure. (CCC: 2351)

Modesty is decency in dress, speech, and manner. Decency may vary according to cultural norms, but in general indecency is any act or communication that arouses sexual feelings in another person outside the marriage relationship. (CCC: 2522-2525)

By *masturbation* is to be understood the deliberate stimulation of the genital organs in order to derive sexual pleasure. (CCC: 2352)

Pornography consists in removing real or simulated sexual acts from the intimacy of the partners, in order to display them deliberately to third parties. (CCC: 2354)

Prostitution does injury to the dignity of the person who engages in it, reducing the person to an instrument of sexual pleasure. (CCC: 2355)

Sodomy is any unnatural coupling (copulation), usually between members of the same sex. The Catechism refers to masturbation, homosexual practices, fornication, and pornography as "sins gravely contrary to chastity." (CCC: 2396)

Notes

Notes